Lenten-Easter Sourcebook

Lenten-Easter Sourcebook

Charles L. Wallis
Editor

ABINGDON PRESS
New York   Nashville

LENTEN-EASTER SOURCEBOOK

Copyright © 1961 by Abingdon Press

Library of Congress Card Number: 61-5200

SET UP, PRINTED, AND BOUND BY THE
PARTHENON PRESS, AT NASHVILLE,
TENNESSEE, UNITED STATES OF AMERICA

Special acknowledgment is made to the following who have granted permission for the reprinting of copyrighted material from the books listed below:

ABINGDON PRESS for extract from *Love Speaks from the Cross* by Leslie Badham, copyright 1955 by Pierce & Washabaugh; extract from *I Believe in Immortality* by John Sutherland Bonnell, copyright © 1959 by Abingdon Press; extracts from *Lift Up Your Hearts* by Walter Russell Bowie, copyright © 1939, 1956 by Pierce & Washabaugh; extracts from *Christ and Man's Dilemma* by George A. Buttrick, copyright 1946 by Stone & Pierce; extract from *Sermons Preached in a University Church* by George A. Buttrick, copyright © 1959 by Abingdon Press; extract from *The Redeemer* by William R. Cannon, copyright 1951 by Pierce & Smith; extract from *The American Pulpit Series* (IV) by William O. Carrington, copyright 1945 by Whitmore & Stone; extract from *The Seven Words* by Clovis G. Chappell, copyright 1952 by Pierce & Smith; extracts from *The Years of Our Lord* by Charles M. Crowe, copyright 1955 by Pierce & Washabaugh; prayer from *Prayers for Christian Services* by Carl A. Glover, copyright © 1959 by Abingdon Press; poem, "After Easter," from *Be Still and Know* by Georgia Harkness, copyright 1953 by Pierce & Washabaugh; poem, "Prayer on Good Friday," from *The Glory of God* by Georgia Harkness, copyright 1943 by Whitmore & Stone; extract from *Abundant Living* by E. Stanley Jones, copyright 1942 by Whitmore & Stone; extract from *Victorious Living* by E. Stanley Jones, copyright 1936 by E. Stanley Jones; extract from *The Lion and the Lamb* by Gerald Kennedy, copyright 1950 by Pierce and Smith; extract from *The Interpreter's Bible* by Halford E. Luccock, copyright 1951 by Pierce & Smith; extract from *What Jesus Really Taught* by Clarence Macartney, copyright © 1958 by Abingdon Press; extract from *Fight the Good Fight* by Robert Menzies, copyright 1951 by Pierce & Smith; extract from *The Hard Commands of Jesus* by Roy Pearson, copyright © 1957 by Abingdon Press; extract from *The Cross and Great Living* by William E. Phifer, Jr., copyright 1943 by Whitmore & Stone; extract from *With Christ in the Garden* by Lynn James Radcliffe, copyright © 1959 by Abingdon Press; extract from *Invitation to Worship* by A. C. Reid, copyright 1942

4

by Whitmore & Stone; prayer from *Pastoral Prayers for the Church Year* by Samuel John Schmiechen, copyright © 1957 by Abingdon Press; extracts from *New Light from Old Lamps* by Roy L. Smith, copyright 1953 by Pierce & Washabaugh; extract from *The Higher Happiness* by Ralph Sockman, copyright 1950 by Pierce & Smith; extracts from *The Life and Teaching of Jesus Christ* by James S. Stewart; extracts from *Daily Meditations on the Seven Last Words* by G. Ernest Thomas, copyright © 1959 by Abingdon Press; prayers from *A Book of Pastoral Prayers* by Ernest Fremont Tittle, copyright 1951 by Pierce & Smith; extract from *A Plain Man Looks at the Cross* by Leslie D. Weatherhead, copyright 1945 by Whitmore & Stone; extract from *Over His Own Signature* by Leslie D. Weatherhead, copyright © 1955 by Pierce & Washabaugh; extract from *Conquering the Seven Deadly Sins* by Lance Webb, copyright 1955 by Pierce & Washabaugh.

ASSOCIATION PRESS for extracts from *Rediscovering the Bible* by Bernhard W. Anderson; extract from *Did Jesus Rise from the Dead?* by James Martin; prayer from *A Face to the Sky* by George Stewart.

AUGSBURG PUBLISHING HOUSE for extract and prayer from *When God Gave Easter* by Gerhard E. Lenski; extract from *Gethsemane to Calvary* by Olin S. Reigstad.

AUGUSTANA BOOK CONCERN for extract from *Passion Perspectives* by G. Erik Hagg; extract from *Sermons on the Passion of Christ* by Martin Luther, tr. by E. Smid and J. T. Isensee.

BAKER BOOK HOUSE for extract from *The Voice from the Cross* by Andrew W. Blackwood, pp. 53 ff., copyright 1957 by the publisher.

BELLWOAR, RICH AND MANKAS and Estate of Jennie Mai Newton for two prayers from *Altar Stairs* by Joseph Fort Newton.

THE BETHANY PRESS for extract from *Thinking Where Jesus Thought* by Hillyer H. Straton, copyright 1945 by C. D. Pantle for the Christian Board of Publication.

BROADMAN PRESS for poem, "Before Pilate," from *With All Thy Heart* by Leslie Savage Clark; extracts from *The Crucifiers—Then and Now* by Talmage C. Johnson.

CAMBRIDGE UNIVERSITY PRESS for extract from *The Disciple* by T. R. Glover.

CHRISTIAN ADVOCATE for "Barabbas Speaks" by Leslie Savage Clark. Reprinted by permission from the *Christian Advocate* (March 4, 1943) Copyright 1943 by Whitmore & Stone.

THE CHRISTIAN CENTURY for "If Any Man Would" by Edwin McNeill Poteat, copyright 1939 by Christian Century Foundation, reprinted by permission from *The Christian Century;* "The Cross" by Adelaide Love, copyright 1945 by Christian Century Foundation, reprinted by permission from *The Christian Century;* "Eden and Gethsemane" by Leslie Savage Clark and "Lent" by Edith Lovejoy Pierce, copyright 1949 by Christian Century Foundation, reprinted by permission from *The Christian Century;* "The Stone Rolled Away" by Elinor Lennen and "Maundy Thursday" by Edith Lovejoy Pierce, copyright 1952 by Christian Century Foundation, reprinted by permission from *The Christian Century;* "Lenten Fare" by Leslie Savage Clark, copyright 1954 by Christian Century Foundation, reprinted by permission from *The Christian Century;* "As Peter Loved" by Jean Hogan Dudley and "On Ash Wednesday" by Elinor Lennen, copyright 1957 by Christian Century Foundation, reprinted by permission from *The Christian Century.*

DOUBLEDAY & COMPANY, INC. for extract from *Peace With God,* copyright 1953 by Billy Graham. Reprinted by permission of Doubleday and Company, Inc.

WM. B. EERDMANS PUBLISHING COMPANY for extract from *Remember Jesus Christ* by Charles Erdman.

THE EPWORTH PRESS for extract from *Christ and His Cross* by W. Russell Maltby.

FABER AND FABER, LTD. for extract from *Who Moved the Stone?* by Frank Morison.

FRIENDSHIP PRESS for poem from *The Cross Is Lifted* by Chandran Devanesen.

5

HARPER & BROTHERS for prayer from *Adventures in Prayer* by Charles Henry Brent; prayer from *Finding God in a New World* by William Adams Brown; scriptural outline of Holy Week from *The Passion Week* by Walter E. Bundy; extract from *The Evanston Report* by W. A. Visser 't Hooft; extracts from *Christ and the Christian* by Nels F. S. Ferré; extract from *The Christian Faith* by Nels F. S. Ferré; extract from *Living Under Tension* by Harry Emerson Fosdick; extract from *On Being a Real Person* by Harry Emerson Fosdick; extract from *The Power to See It Through* by Harry Emerson Fosdick; prayer from *Prayers for Special Days and Occasions,* ed. by G. B. F. Hallock; extract from *Meditations on the Cross* by Toyohiko Kagawa; extract from *Christ the Lord* by John Knox; extract from *Let Us Keep Lent* by Gerhard E. Lenski; extract from *If God Be for Us* by Robert E. Luccock; extract and prayers from *Joyous Adventure* by David A. MacLennen; extract from *Questions People Ask* by Robert J. McCracken; prayers from *Prayers for Daily Use* by Samuel H. Miller; prayers by Wallace Petty and James D. Morrison from *Minister's Service Book,* ed. by James D. Morrison; extract from sermon by Harry Emerson Fosdick in *Great Preaching Today,* ed. by Alton M. Motter; extract from *His Cross and Ours* by Joseph Fort Newton; extracts from *The Sword of the Spirit* by Joseph Fort Newton; extracts from *That They May Have Life* by Daniel T. Niles; prayer from *Communion With God* by Elmore McNeill McKee; "Barabbas Speaks" and "Palm Sunday and Monday" from *Over the Sea the Sky* by Edwin McNeill Poteat; extract from *The Best of Dick Sheppard,* ed. by Halford E. Luccock; extract from *Sermons Preached at Harvard* by Willard L. Sperry; extract from *One Fine Hour* by Frederick K. Stamm; "Gambler" from *The Unutterable Beauty* by G. A. Studdert-Kennedy, copyright by Harper & Brothers, reprinted by permission; extract from *Our Common Loyalty* by Philemon F. Sturges; prayers from *Prayers of the Spirit* by John Wallace Suter; extract from *His Last Week* by J. W. G. Ward; extracts from *We Are Able* by Luther A. Weigle.

HODDER & STOUGHTON, LTD. for extracts from *In The Days of the Cross* by W. M. Clow; extract from *Social Aspects of the Cross* by Henry Sloane Coffin; extracts from *Footsteps in the Path of Life* by Marcus Dods; prayer and extracts from *Seven Words* by W. R. Matthews; extract from *The Footsteps of the Flock* by George H. Morrison; extract from *The Gateways of the Stars* by George H. Morrison; extract from *The Weaving of Glory* by George H. Morrison; extract from *The Wind on the Heath* by George H. Morrison.

HOUGHTON MIFFLIN COMPANY for extract from *The Living Faith* by Lloyd C. Douglas.

HYMN SOCIETY OF AMERICA for "Above the Hills of Time" and extract from "When the Day Wanes," copyright by Thomas Tiplady. Used by permission of the Hymn Society of America.

INDEPENDENT PRESS, LTD. for extracts from *Lord of All* by John Trevor Davies.

THE JUDSON PRESS for extract from *The Master Purpose of Jesus* by John D. Rhoades. Copyright 1929, The Judson Press. Used by permission. Extract from *And So I Preached This!* by Luther Wesley Smith. Copyright 1936, The Judson Press. Used by permission.

J. B. LIPPINCOTT COMPANY for extract from *A Book of Days for Christians* by Richardson Wright.

LONGMANS, GREEN & COMPANY, INC. for "The Cross" and "At Emmaus" from *A Rime of the Rood and Other Poems* by Charles L. O'Donnell.

LUTTERWORTH PRESS for extract from *The Mediator* by Emil Brunner, tr. by Olive Wyon.

THE MACMILLAN COMPANY for extract from *The Cross and the Eternal Order* by Henry W. Clark; quotation by Lloyd C. Douglas from *Behold the Man;* extract from *Christ's Victory and Ours* by Frederick C. Grant; extracts from *The Passion of the*

King by Frederick C. Grant, copyright 1955 by The Macmillan Company, reprinted by permission; extract from *Pathways to the Reality of God* by Rufus M. Jones; extract from *Suffering, Human and Divine* by H. Wheeler Robinson; extracts from *In the Shadow of the Cross* by Frederick K. Stamm.

MOREHOUSE-BARLOW COMPANY, INC. for extract and prayer from *The Cross, Our Hope* by J. Wilson Sutton; extract from *Were You There?* by Harold E. Wagner.

MUHLENBERG PRESS for extract from *Eucharist and Sacrifice* by Gustaf Aulén, tr. Eric H. Wahlstrom; extract from sermon by John W. Rilling in *Keeping Lent*, ed. Paul Z. Strodach; extracts from sermons by Oscar F. Blackwelder and Theodore K. Finck from *But Christ Did Rise!*, ed. by Paul Z. Strodach; extracts from sermons by Carl R. Simon and Louis A. Sittler from *Victim or Victor*, ed. by Paul Z. Strodach.

JAMES NISBET AND COMPANY for extract from *The Healing Cross* by H. H. Farmer.

OXFORD UNIVERSITY PRESS, INC. for extract from *The Story of Jesus* by Theodore P. Ferris.

OXFORD UNIVERSITY PRESS, LTD. for extracts from *Jesus of Nazareth* by Charles Gore; prayer from *Divine Service* by W. E. Orchard.

PULPIT DIGEST for extracts from sermons by Ralph S. Barber and Samuel McCrea Cavert from *Pulpit Digest;* prayer from *In His Name* by G. A. Cleveland Shrigley, published by the Pulpit Press.

RAND McNALLY & COMPANY for extract from "Gethsemane" by Ella Wheeler Wilcox.

THE REILLY & LEE COMPANY for "Ash Wednesday" from *Living the Years* by Edgar A. Guest. Copyright 1949, The Reilly & Lee Company.

FLEMING H. REVELL COMPANY for extract from *Road to Radiant Living* by Charles L. Allen; extract from *Christ's Service of Love* by Hugh Black; extract from *The Kingdom Is Yours* by Louis H. Evans; prayers from *A Book of Invocations* by Herman Paul Guhsé; extract and prayer from *Mr. Jones, Meet the Master* by Peter Marshall; prayer from *A Prayer for Every Day* by John Lewis Sandlin; extract from *Pulpit and Parish Manual* by Henry Hallam Saunderson; extracts from *Christ's Words from the Cross* by Samuel Shoemaker.

CHARLES SCRIBNER'S SONS for extract from *Invitation to Pilgrimage* by John Baillie and by permission of Oxford University Press; extract from *God Confronts Man in History* by Henry Sloane Coffin; extracts from *Joy in Believing* by Henry Sloane Coffin, copyright © 1956 Dorothy Prentice Coffin. Extracts from *The Meaning of the Cross* by Henry Sloane Coffin, copyright 1931 Charles Scribner's Sons; renewal copyright 1959 Dorothy Prentice Coffin. Prayer by Georgia Harkness from *Pastoral Prayers Through the Year* compiled and edited by Robert L. Eddy, copyright © 1959 Robert L. Eddy. Extract from *Sermons* by H. R. Mackintosh: extract from *High Country* by Alistair MacLean, copyright 1952 Charles Scribner's Sons. Extract from *Beyond Tragedy* by Reinhold Niebuhr; extract from *Faith and History* by Reinhold Niebuhr, copyright 1949 Charles Scribner's Sons and by permission of James Nisbet and Company. Extract from *Modern Man and the Cross* by John C. Schroeder; extract from *The Gates of New Life* by James S. Stewart and by permission of T. & T. Clark; extract from *The Strong Name* by James S. Stewart and by permission of T. & T. Clark; extract from *The New Being* by Paul Tillich and by permission of Student Christian Movement Press.

THE SEABURY PRESS for extract from *Christian Living* by Stephen F. Bayne, Jr.; extract from *Christ Speaks from the Cross* by Gardiner M. Day; extracts from *By Means of Death* by Hughell E. W. Fosbroke; extracts from *Jesus and His Ministry* by Wallace Eugene Rollins and Marion Benedict Rollins.

STUDENT CHRISTIAN MOVEMENT PRESS, LTD. for extract from *Jesus in the Experience of Men* by T. R. Glover.

THE UPPER ROOM for extracts from sermons by H. E. D. Ashford, Jesse M. Bader,

7

Clarence W. Cranford, I. W. Gernert, G. Ray Jordan, Edward Hughes Pruden, John Short, and C. H. Stauffacher, and "Meditation for Holy Communion" by Russell Q. Chilcote from *The Upper Room Pulpit.*

THE WESTMINSTER PRESS for extract from *The Gospel of Mark* by William Barclay. Published in 1957 by The Westminster Press, reprinted by permission of The Westminster Press and The Saint Andrew Press. Extract from *The Practice and Power of Prayer* by John Sutherland Bonnell. Copyright 1954 by W. L. Jenkins, reprinted by permission of The Westminster Press. Extract from *Jesus Christ and His Cross* by F. W. Dillistone. Copyright 1953 by W. L. Jenkins, reprinted by permission of The Westminster Press and Lutterworth Press. Extract from *Introducing New Testament Theology* by A. M. Hunter. Published in 1957 by The Westminster Press, reprinted by permission of the Westminster Press and Student Christian Movement Press. Extract from *The Inward Cross* by Charles Duell Kean. Copyright 1952 by W. L. Jenkins, reprinted by permission of The Westminster Press. Extract from *Meditations from Kierkegaard,* ed. by T. H. Croxall. Copyright 1955 by W. L. Jenkins, reprinted by permission of The Westminster Press and James Nisbet and Company, Ltd. Extract from *The Resurrection of Christ* by A. Michael Ramsey. Copyright 1955 by W. L. Jenkins, reprinted by permission of The Westminster Press and Geoffrey Bles, Ltd. Extract from *The Unity of the Bible* by H. H. Rowley. Published 1955, reprinted by permission of The Westminster Press and The Carey Kingsgate Press, Ltd.

ZONDERVAN PUBLISHING HOUSE for extract from *The Cross Athwart the Sky* by R. E. Golladay.

Special acknowledgment is also made to the following persons for permission to reprint the materials indicated:

MARGARET E. BRUNER for "Joseph of Arimathaea" from *Midstream.*

LESLIE SAVAGE CLARK for "Palm Sunday" and "Before Pilate."

G. RAY JORDAN for extracts from *Why the Cross.*

BARBARA LOWRIE for extract from *The Short Story of Jesus* by Walter Lowrie.

J. T. MORELAND for "Christ Is Crucified Anew" and "If a Man Die" by John R. Moreland.

IDA NORTON MUNSON for "Easter Light" from *Journeys in Poetry* and "The Road to Emmaus" from *The Surgeon's Hands.*

JAMES J. HAYES for extract from *The Resurrection Fact* by Doremus A. Hayes

O. P. KRETZMANN and ARMIN C. OLDSEN for extracts from *Voices of the Passion.*

THEO OXENHAM for "He—They—We" and extract from "The Key" from *Selected Poems of John Oxenham,* ed. by Charles L. Wallis.

JOHNSTONE G. PATRICK for "Good Friday" and "A Loaf of Bread, a Jug of Wine, and a Towel" from *Above the Thorn.*

HAROLD C. PHILLIPS for extract from *In the Light of the Cross.*

JAMES REID for extract from *Facing Life With Christ.*

MARY S. ROBBINS for "Via Lucis" by Howard Chandler Robbins.

EDITH G. SCHLOERB for "Around the Brow of Olivet" by Rolland W. Schloerb.

HAROLD A. SCHULZ for "Cinquin: I Too Was Born."

RALPH W. SEAGER for "Spring Belongs With Easter" from *Songs from a Willow Whistle.*

ELEANOR SLATER for "Yet More Than All" from *Why Hold the Hound?*

T. F. TORRENCE for extract from *Scottish Journal of Theology.*

VIOLET ALLEYN STOREY from "After Calvary" and "And He Was Only Thirty-Three."

ERNEST A. WALL for extract from *The Sovereign Emblem.*

To

William S. Litterick

Preface

This book has been prepared as a homiletic and worship resource volume for pastors and church workers. The materials reflect the mind and heart of main-stream Christianity throughout many centuries and emphasize the varied facets of the passion and resurrection of our Lord. Many voices which speak with persuasion and verve to the needs and aspirations, the fears and hopes, of our generation have been identified.

The celebration of Easter, the magnetic heart of the gospel proclamation, began in the worship practices of the Apostles. Holy Week was observed in the early church. The custom of keeping Lent dates to ancient times and has generally been thought of as an appropriate period of penitence and prayer in anticipation of Easter.

Lent means many things to many people. Though not consistently observed within evangelical Christianity, this period of grace offers a privilege, available as in no other season, for the heightening of spiritual ministries and the deepening of the spiritual life. How ever the season may be commemorated, we ought not to bypass such advantages as accrue at a time when the Christian community is especially sensitive to and prepared to accept the good news.

A seventeenth century proverb says, "Easter so longed for is gone in a day." The churches frequently experience a post-Easter lethargy. This results in part from a magnification of the central emphases of the gospel message during Lent and on Easter and a subsequent diminishing of perspective in regard to the relative role of other days and seasons. John Keble said of Easter:

> Thou art the Sun of other days,
> They shine by giving back thy rays.

The other days should shine, too, and they will if we remember that the primitive church did not think only of Easter as the day of resurrection. Rather, each Lord's day was a single occasion for remembering that Jesus Christ "hath abolished death, and hath brought life and

11

immortality to light through the gospel" and that according to his abundant mercy we are "begotten again unto a lively hope." This book, prepared particularly for seasonal use, contains materials which properly belong to the entire Christian year.

CHARLES L. WALLIS

Contents

I. Holy Week:
A Scriptural Outline[1]

PALM SUNDAY

	MATTHEW	MARK	LUKE
1. The Bethany demonstration[2]	21:1-9	11:1-10	19:29-38
2. The protest of the Pharisees[3]	21:15-16	...	19:39-40
3. The prophecy of the fall of Jerusalem	...	...	19:41-44
4. The entry into the Holy City	21:10-11	11:11	...
5. In the Temple: Observations	21:12	11:11	19:45
6. The cleansing of the Temple[4]	21:12-13	11:15-17	19:45-46
7. The blind and lame cured in the Temple	21:14	...	...
8. The protest of the chief priests	21:15-16	...	19:39-40
9. The return to Bethany	21:17	11:11	...

MONDAY

	MATTHEW	MARK	LUKE
1. The cursing of the fig tree	21:18-19	11:12-14	13:6-19; 17:6
2. The cleansing of the Temple[5]	21:12-13	11:15-17	19:45-46

[1] Based on Walter E. Bundy, *The Passion Week.*
[2] John 12:12-18.
[3] John 12:19.
[4] John 2:13-17.
[5] John 2:13-17.

17

	MATTHEW	MARK	LUKE
3. The chief priests and the scribes	21:15-16	11:18	19:47-48
4. Jesus lodges outside the city	. . .	11:19	21:37

TUESDAY

	MATTHEW	MARK	LUKE
1. The withered fig tree	21:20	11:20-21	. . .
2. Faith in God and prayer	21:21-22; 17:20	11:22-25	17:6
3. The question of Jesus' authority	21:23-27	11:27-33	20:1-8
4. The parable of the two unlike sons	21:28-32	. . .	7:29-30
5. The parable of the wicked husbandmen	21:33-46	12:1-12	20:9-19
6. The parable of the marriage feast	22:1-14	. . .	14:16-24
7. The question of the tribute money	22:15-22	12:13-17	20:20-26
8. The question of the resurrection	22:23-33	12:18-27	20:27-38
9. The question of the great command	22:34-40	12:28-34	20:39-40; 10:25-28
10. The question of David's Messiah	22:41-46	12:35-37	20:41-44
11. Address against scribes and Pharisees	23:1-39	12:38-40	20:45-47; 11:37-54
12. The widow's mites	. . .	12:41-44	21:1-4
13. Prophecy on destruction of the Temple[6]	24:1-2	13:1-2	21:5-6
14. Address on the last things	24:3– 25:46	13:3-37	21:7-36; 17:20-37

[6] John 2:19-22; Matt. 26:61; 27:40; Mark 14:58; 15:29-30.

18

	MATTHEW	MARK	LUKE
15. Jesus lodges outside the city	...	11:19	21:37-38

WEDNESDAY

1. The conspiracy of the chief priests[7]	26:1-5	14:1-2	22:1-2
2. The anointing in Bethany[8]	26:6-13	14:3-9	7:36-50
3. Judas betrays Jesus[9]	26:14-16	14:10-11	22:3-6

THURSDAY

1. The preparation of the Passover	26:17-19	14:12-16	22:7-13

GOOD FRIDAY

SCENE I. *At the Table*[10]

1. At the table with the Twelve[11]	26:20	14:17	22:14
2. The designation of the betrayer[12]	26:21-25	14:18-21	22:21-23
3. The Last Supper (Matt.-Markan text)	26:26-29	14:22-25	...
4. The Passover Cup (Lukan A text)	...	...	22:15-18
5. The Lord's Supper[13] (Paul-Lukan B text)	...	I Cor. 11:23-26	22:19-20;
6. The designation of the betrayer[14]	...	...	22:21-23
7. A contention concerning rank	...	9:33-34	22:24; 9:46
8. Service as the test of greatness	20:25-28	...	22:25-27; 10:42-45

[7] John 11:47-53.
[8] John 12:1-8.
[9] John 13:2, 27.
[10] John 13-17.

[11] John 13:1-9.
[12] John 13:10-11, 21-30.
[13] John 6:52-59.
[14] John 13:10-11, 21-30.

	MATTHEW	MARK	LUKE
9. Thrones for the Twelve	19:28	...	22:28-30
10. Special supplication for Simon	......	......	22:31-32
11. Peter's pledge: his denial foretold	26:33-35	14:29-31	22:33-34
12. Purse and sword	......	...... 10:4;	22:35-38
13. On the way to Gethsemane	26:30-32	14:26-28	22:39

SCENE II. *Gethsemane*[15]

	MATTHEW	MARK	LUKE
1. Jesus' personal struggle	26:36-46	14:32-42	22:40-46
2. The arrest [16]	26:47-50	14:43-46	22:47-48, 54
3. The resistance[17]	26:51-54	14:47	22:49-51
4. The healing of the severed ear	......	......	22:51
5. Jesus' remonstrance[18]	26:55-56	14:48-49	22:52-53
6. The desertion of the Disciples[19]	26:56	14:50	......
7. The flight of a certain young man	......	14:51-52	......

SCENE III. *The Jewish Trial*[20]

	MATTHEW	MARK	LUKE
1. The delivery to the high priest [21]	26:57-58	14:53-54	22:54-55
2. The Jewish trial *at night* [22]	26:59-66	14:55-64	22:67-71
3. Jesus mocked *after* the Jewish trial [23]	26:67-68	14:65	22:63-65
4. Peter's denial [24]	26:69-75	14:66-72	22:56-62

[15] John 18:1-11.
[16] John 18:1-8, 12.
[17] John 18:10-11, 26.
[18] John 18:19-21.
[19] John 18:8-9.

[20] John 18:12-28.
[21] John 18:12-14, 24.
[22] John 18:19-21; 19:7.
[23] John 18:22-24.
[24] John 18:15-18, 25-27.

	Matthew	Mark	Luke
5. Jesus mocked *before* the Jewish trial [25]	26:67-68	14:65	22:63-65
6. The Jewish trial *at dawn* [26]	26:63-66	14:61-64	22:66-67
7. The delivery to Pilate [27]	27:1-2	15:1	23:1
8. The remorse and suicide of Judas	27:3-10	......	Acts 1:16-20

Scene IV. *The Roman Trial* [28]

	Matthew	Mark	Luke
1. Jesus before Pilate [29]	27:11-14	15:2-5	23:2-3
2. Pilate declares Jesus innocent [30]	......	......	23:4
3. The delivery to Herod [31]	......	......	23:5-7
4. Jesus before Herod [32]	27:28-30	15:17-19	23:8-12
5. Before Pilate again: 2nd declaration [33]	......	......	23:13-16
6. The Passover amnesty: Barabbas [34]	27:15-18	15:6-10	23:18-19
7. The intervention of Pilate's wife	27:19	......	......
8. Request for Barabbas: 3rd declaration [35]	27:20-23	15:11-14	23:18-23
9. Pilate washes his hands	27:24-25	......	......
10. Barabbas released; Jesus condemned [36]	27:26	15:15	23:23-25
11. Jesus mocked by the Roman soldiers [37]	27:27-31	15:16-20	23:11

Scene V. *The Crucifixion* [38]

	Matthew	Mark	Luke
1. Simon of Cyrene [39]	27:32	15:21	23:26
2. *Via Dolorosa*	......	......	23:27-31

[25] John 18:22-24.
[26] John 18:19-21; 19:7.
[27] John 18:28.
[28] John 18:29–19:16.
[29] John 18:29-32, 33-38; 19:8-11.
[30] John 18:38; 19:4, 6.
[31] John 18:24.
[32] Acts 4:27-28.

[33] John 19:12-14.
[34] John 18:38-40.
[35] John 19:4-7, 14-15; Acts 3:13-14.
[36] John 19:1, 16.
[37] John 19:2-3.
[38] John 19:17-42.
[39] John 19:17.

	MATTHEW	MARK	LUKE
3. The crucifixion[40]	27:33-35	15:22-25	23:32-34
4. Jesus mocked at the Cross[41]	27:36-44	15:26-32	23:35-39
5. The malefactor on the cross	. . . . . .	. . . . . .	23:40-43
6. The death of Jesus[42]	27:45-50	15:33-37	23:44-46
7. Attendant signs	27:51-53	15:38	23:45
8. The centurion at the cross	27:54	15:39	23:47
9. The grief of the multitudes	. . . . . .	. . . . . .	23:48
10. The Galilean women as witnesses[43]	27:55-56	15:40-41	8:1-3; 23:49
11. The burial of Jesus[44]	27:57-60	15:42-46	23:50-54
12. The Galilean women as witnesses	27:61	15:47	23:55-56
13. The watch at the sepulcher	27:62-66	. . . . . .	. . . . . .

[40] John 19:17-18, 23-25.
[41] John 19:19-22.
[42] John 19:28-37.
[43] John 19:25-27.
[44] John 19:38-42.

22

II. Period of Preparation

1. OBSERVING LENT

The observance of Lent, and the other seasons of the Church Year, is by no means universal. Many devout Christians believe that no special day for worship has divine sanction, excepting the weekly Sabbath. Nor is the observance uniform; some churches prescribe an extended and intricate round of saints' days, of fasts and feasts, to which almost every day of the calendar is in some way related; others limit their festivals exclusively to Christmas and Easter.

Nor is the observance obligatory. Freedom of choice should be allowed. The words of Paul must be regarded. "One man esteemeth one day above another: another esteemeth every day alike. Let every man be fully persuaded in his own mind" (Romans 14:5). Therefore, as the apostle further intimates, one who observes the demands of a most exacting Church Year should not be regarded as bound by narrow tradition, nor should one who disregards such demands be considered irreverent or lacking in faith.

Some observance of Christian anniversaries will certainly be found helpful and quite in accordance with Scripture and human needs. By these seasons the memorable events in the life of Christ are brought to mind; otherwise they might be neglected; then, too, it is inspiring to know that the same great realities are being remembered at the same time by countless Christians in all parts of the world. Thus a Christian Year may result in bringing more closely together all the members of the "Body of Christ."

CHARLES R. ERDMAN

2. SPIRITUAL SIGNIFICANCE OF LENT

What is the spiritual significance of Lent? It has been for generations a common practice among non-ritualistic Protestants to speak and think lightly of Lent. Is it not one of those superstitious practices, one of those meaningless institutions born of dogma in the dark ages when the Christian church was dominated by Rome? What care we for this bit of medievalism? Let us be what we are going to be the year 'round, we say. What is the sense in refraining from doing during part of the year what we propose to do throughout the rest of the year, unless what we give up doing ought not to be done anyway? Thinking thus we are tempted to toss aside lightly with the incrustment of the institution the spiritual truth which gave it birth, the significance of which we ought to hold steadily and unremittingly before our eyes and thoughts during these days.

There are several special forty-day periods in biblically recorded experience. One was when Moses went to the mountain to fast and pray; and at the conclusion of that experience there came to him by way of flashing insight and revelation the understanding of the moral law which is set down in what we call the Ten Commandments. Another such period was when Elijah withdrew to the cave in the side of Mount Horeb. Another was that recorded in the experience of Jesus following his baptism. At the climax of this experience came the temptation.

Each of these periods was one of fasting and prayer, of self-discipline and self-denial. Each period was charged with some great spiritual experience. So the leaders of the early church, realizing what such a period meant to Christ, called upon the people to set aside the forty days preceding the commemoration of Easter, giving themselves during these forty days—plus six Sundays—to meditation and self-denial, to the end that they, too, might enter truly and fully into the spiritual exaltation of the Easter truth, the climactic truth of the Christian faith.

Because of the self-denial which Jesus practised during the days when he drew apart to meditate and pray, and because of the self-denial to which he called his disciples in ringing challenges during the days immediately preceding his crucifixion, it is natural, indeed inevitable, that Lent in our thinking should become associated with self-denial. The starting-point of the spiritual significance of Lent is its reminder of the insistence of Jesus that self-denial is the path to self-realization.

LUTHER WESLEY SMITH

24

3. PRIMARY CONCERN

Lent . . . is primarily a time of preparation. That was its origin, long centuries ago, when the season came into existence because of the need of the new converts for training and education in the new duties which they were to assume at their baptism and confirmation at Eastertide. Even though we no longer restrict Christian initiation to Eastertide, the Church has clung to the six weeks of the annual school, because we knew that it was needed not only by the new converts but certainly by the old-timers as well.

This is still the best way for us to approach Lent and understand it. What we do in Lent—the discipline we undertake—ought to be calculated in the light of that purpose. What do we need in order that we may be better trained, more free, more obedient to serve our Lord?

The negative aspects of Lent are incidental to this purpose. We abstain from the common amusements and pleasures of life during Lent not because there is something evil in them, but because by so abstaining *we set ourselves free for our primary concern.* If our pleasures and relaxations were evil, then we ought never to indulge in them. But they are not evil, but good; yet there are more important things; and Lent is a time for putting first things first.

Stephen F. Bayne, Jr.

4. WHY WE KEEP LENT

"The most awful thing in the death of Jesus," Archbishop Söderblom reminds us, "is that it was brought about by men who were following or believed themselves to be following good and honorable reasons for their actions. Men of various classes, the guardians of religion and of public morals and of the order of society itself united to crucify Jesus. They were men like you and me." That is why we keep Lent. That is why the Church lifts up her voice and calls all Christians to repentance. "Turn ye even to me with all your heart, and with fasting and with weeping and with mourning." There is an old Passion hymn, a great favorite in Luther's day, that opens with the question, "O thou wretched Judas, what hast thou now done?" Fortunately the hymn is no longer sung, for as Luther pointed out it tends to keep the Passion back in a by-gone day as though it were none of our affair. More to the point is the personal and deeply penitent confession of that other Passion chorale, "Who was the guilty, who brought this upon Thee, alas *my* treason, Jesus, hath undone Thee." He was wounded for *our* transgressions.

JOHN W. RILLING

5. LENT

Here is the hill. Let us begin the climb
Into clear air, and into cloudless light.
Breath on hard breath, measuring hours by height,
And in the slow ascent transforming time.

Seen from this mountain is no devil's view:
The kingdoms of the world are all God's own.
Him we must worship. In this crystal zone
We see more clearly what we never knew.

And with perspective we the fiend outface.
Sky is less changed than earth by altitude,
Less changed than life; by the new heart construed
Earth's pale geography falls into place.

EDITH LOVEJOY PIERCE

6. LENTEN FARE

Now let the body fast a while,
The shelf and board grow lean,
And man lift up his hungry heart
To find a world unseen.

Now let him know his beggared state,
What starveling fare is bread,
What sparse and bitter herbs are his
Unless the soul be fed.

LESLIE SAVAGE CLARK

26

7. SPIRITUAL FOCUS

Self-denial, for the sake of self-denial, does no good; self-sacrifice for its own sake is no religious act at all. If you give up a meal for the sake of showing power over self, or for the sake of self-discipline, it is the most miserable of all delusions. You are not more religious in doing this than before. This is mere self-culture; and self-culture, being occupied forever about self, leaves you only in that circle of self from which religion is to free you; but to give up a meal that one you love may have it, is properly a religious act—no hard and dismal duty, because made easy by affection. To bear pain for the sake of bearing it has in it no moral quality at all; but to bear it rather than surrender truth, or in order to save another, is positive enjoyment, as well as ennobling to the soul.

FREDERICK W. ROBERTSON

8. ON ASH WEDNESDAY

Ashes are everywhere, to mock the pride
That raged and leaped and perished in its flame,
Yet vanity within us has not died;
The cautery has left us much the same.

Before our bones are ashes, and our wills
Have forfeited all power to repent,
God, bend our stubborn spirits and our skills
To uttermost obedience this Lent!

ELINOR LENNEN

9. ASH WEDNESDAY

Time was to church the faithful went,
Repenting every sinful fall.
The priest towards their foreheads bent
And crossed with ashes one and all.

This was a symbol to proclaim
The faithful sorrowed for their sins.

27

From this Ash Wednesday got its name—
The holy day when Lent begins.

Still from all worldly pleasures gay
    The faithful vow to turn aside,
In preparation for the day
    He rose who had been crucified.

Lent! when the faithful kneel to pray
    For strength to live as they believe,
A little braver through the day;
    A little quieter at eve.

EDGAR A. GUEST

III. Themes for Lenten Preaching

A. 100 TOPICS AND TEXTS

10. IF JESUS HAD NOT COME
If I had not come and spoken to them. (JOHN 15:22 Moffatt.)

11. FAITH FOR MAXIMUM LIVING
And the apostles said unto the Lord, Increase our faith. (LUKE 17:5.)

12. THE PERSPECTIVES OF LOVE
As the Father hath loved me, so have I loved you: continue ye in my love. (JOHN 15:9.)

13. CHRIST WITHIN THE FAMILY CIRCLE
Abide with us: for it is toward evening, and the day is far spent. (LUKE 24:29.)

14. RELUCTANT DISCIPLES
And he answered and said, I go, sir: and went not. (MATT. 21:30.)

15. THE UNATTRACTIVE CROSS
Most men's love will grow cold. (MATT. 24:12 RSV.)

16. CONFRONTING CHRIST IN CONTEMPORARY EXPERIENCE
Lord, to whom shall we go? Thou hast the words of eternal life. (JOHN 6:68.)

17. CHRIST COMPELLED BY A PURPOSE
To this end was I born, and for this cause came I into the world, that I should bear witness unto the truth. (JOHN 18:37.)

18. LIPS THAT AFFIRM AND HEARTS THAT DENY
And the multitudes . . . cried, saying, Hosanna to the son of

David. (MATT. 21:9.) And they cried out again, Crucify him. (MARK 15:13.)

19. GOALS TOWARD WHICH WE STRIVE
He stedfastly set his face to go to Jerusalem. (LUKE 9:51.)

20. THE PERILS OF SPIRITUAL TRUANCY
But Thomas . . . was not with them when Jesus came. (JOHN 20:24.)

21. THE SENSITIVITY OF JESUS
When he was come near, he beheld the city, and wept over it. (LUKE 19:41.)

22. PALM-WAVING CHRISTIANS
When they heard that Jesus was coming to Jerusalem, [they] took branches of palm trees, and went forth to meet him. (JOHN 12:12-13.)

23. KING FOR MORE THAN A DAY
Behold your King! (JOHN 19:14.)

24. REST AMID TENSIONS
And at night he went out, and abode in the mount that is called the mount of Olives. (LUKE 21:37.)

25. SPECTATOR DISCIPLESHIP
Sit ye here, while I shall pray. (MARK 14:32.)

26. VIGILENCE THE PRICE OF SPIRITUAL ACHIEVEMENT
Watch and pray, that ye enter not into temptation. (MATT. 26:41.)

27. SLEEPING THROUGH A CRISIS
Could ye not watch with me one hour? (MATT. 26:40.)

28. HOMES WHERE CHRIST IS WELCOMED
Where is the guestchamber, where I shall eat the passover with my disciples? (LUKE 22:11.)

29. CHRIST AS COMRADE
I have longed eagerly to eat this passover with you. (LUKE 22:15.)

30. A NIGHT TO REMEMBER
   The same night in which he was betrayed. (I Cor. 11:23.)

31. A LESSON IN HUMILITY
   But I am among you as he that serveth. (Luke 22:27.)

32. MEMORIES WHICH OBLIGATE CHRISTIANS
   This do in remembrance of me. (I Cor. 11:24.)

33. SELF-EXAMINATION
   Lord, is it I? (Matt. 26:22.)

34. JUDAS CHOSE THE SHADOWS
   He then having received the sop went immediately out: and it was night. (John 13:30.)

35. THE MINISTRIES OF SONG
   When they had sung an hymn, they went out into the mount of Olives. (Matt. 26:30.)

36. BEHOLD THE MAN
   He was in the world . . . and the world did not recognize Him. (John 1:10 Weymouth.)

37. THE STRATAGEMS OF SATAN
   From that day forth they took counsel together for to put him to death. (John 11:53.)

38. THE AUTHORITY OF SILENCE
   But Jesus was silent. (Matt. 26:63 Phillips.)

39. WHEN CHRIST GETS IN OUR WAY
   What shall I do then with Jesus which is called Christ? (Matt. 27:22.)

40. THE QUESTION OF SOVEREIGNTY
   Art thou the King of the Jews? (Matt. 27:11.)

41. THE PUBLIC RECORD
   I spake openly to the world . . . and in secret have I said nothing. (John 18:20.)

42. THE HEART'S TESTIMONY
Sayest thou this thing of thyself, or did others tell it thee of me? (JOHN 18:34.)

43. PILATE: A STUDY IN IRRESPONSIBILITY
Whosoever therefore shall confess me before men, him will I confess also before my Father which is in heaven. (MATT. 10:32.)

44. FATEFUL CHOICES
Not this man, but Barabbas. (JOHN 18:40.)

45. EARTH'S PREVAILING VOICES
And the voices of them and of the chief priests prevailed. (LUKE 23:23.)

46. THE VOICE OF THE PEOPLE OR THE VOICE OF GOD
There are . . . so many kinds of voices in the world. (I COR. 14:10.)

47. MISINTERPRETING JESUS
And some of them that stood by . . . said, Behold, he calleth Elias. (MARK 15:35.)

48. LOVE'S RENDEZVOUS
Judas also . . . knew the place: for Jesus ofttimes resorted thither with his disciples. (JOHN 18:2.)

49. WHOM DO YOU SEEK?
I am he. (JOHN 18:5.)

50. A CHRISTIAN'S ACCENT
Surely thou also art one of them; for thy speech betrayeth thee. (MATT. 26:73.)

51. WEAK-KNEED AFFIRMATIONS
Though I should die with thee, yet will I not deny thee. Likewise also said all the disciples. (MATT. 26:35.)

52. FOLLOWING FROM AFAR
But Peter followed him afar off. (MATT. 26:58.)

53. AWAKENING OF A SLUMBERING CONSCIENCE
And immediately, while he yet spake, the cock crew. (LUKE 22:60.)

54. THE TRANSFORMATION OF SORROW

Your heart is full of sorrow at which I have told you. Yet—I am telling you the truth—my going is for your good. (John 16:6-7 Phillips.)

55. JESUS AS VOLUNTEER OR VICTIM?

No man taketh [my life] from me, but I lay it down of myself. (John 10:18.)

56. THE MAGNETISM OF THE MASTER

I, if I be lifted up from the earth, will draw all men unto me. (John 12:32.)

57. CROSSES WE CANNOT SHRUG OFF

They found a man of Cyrene, Simon by name: him they compelled to bear his cross. (Matt. 27:32.)

58. THE WEIGHT OF A CROSS

On him they laid the cross, that he might bear it after Jesus. (Luke 23:26.)

59. THE FELLOWSHIP OF THE CROSS

If any man will come after me, let him deny himself, and take up his cross daily, and follow me. (Luke 9:23.)

60. THE CORONATION OF SUFFERING

When they had platted a crown of thorns, they put it upon his head. (Matt. 27:29.)

61. THE GEOGRAPHY OF CALVARY

The place where Jesus was crucified was nigh to the city. (John 19:20.)

62. LOVE EMBRACING THE PENITENT THIEF

Of a truth I perceive that God is no respecter of persons. (Acts 10:34.)

63. NONE ARE INNOCENT AT CALVARY

He that is not with me is against me. (Matt. 12:30.)

64. THE APPEAL OF THE SPECTACULAR
    If he be the King of Israel, let him now come down from the cross, and we will believe him. (MATT. 27:42.)

65. BYSTANDERS AT CALVARY
    And sitting down they watched him there. (MATT. 27:36.)

66. THE PROOF OF GOD'S LOVE
    God proves his love for us by this, that Christ died for us when we were still sinners. (Rom. 5:8 Moffatt.)

67. COMING TO TERMS WITH SIN
    Who his own self bare our sins in his own body on the tree. (I PET. 2:24.)

68. THE HIGH COST OF OUR SALVATION
    You have been redeemed, at tremendous cost; don't therefore sell yourselves as slaves to men! (I COR. 7:23 Phillips.)

69. THE ATTRACTION AND REPULSION OF THE CROSS
    We preach Christ crucified, unto the Jews a stumblingblock, and unto the Greeks foolishness; but unto them which are called . . . Christ the power of God, and the wisdom of God. (I COR. 1:23-24.)

70. THE RADIANT CROSS
    They looked unto him, and were lightened. (Ps. 34:5.)

71. THE CROSS: GUIDEPOST OF FAITH
    Many shall come in my name, saying, I am Christ; and shall deceive many. (MATT. 24:5.)

72. CROSS-CENTERED LIVING
    God forbid that I should glory, save in the cross of our Lord Jesus Christ. (GAL. 6:14.)

73. CLOUDS OVER CALVARY
    The Light shines in the darkness, and the darkness has not overpowered it. (JOHN 1:5 Weymouth.)

74. THE UNFINISHED WORK OF JESUS
    It is finished. (JOHN 19:30.)

75. A CENTURION'S CONFESSION
    Truly this man was the Son of God. (MARK 15:39.)

76. A COURAGEOUS COWARD
   Joseph of Arimathaea, being a disciple of Jesus, but secretly for fear of the Jews, besought Pilate. (JOHN 19:38.)

77. DISCIPLES FROM THE SHADOWS
   Nicodemus, which at the first came to Jesus by night. (JOHN 19:39.)

78. LIFE IS NEVER THE SAME
   Simon Peter saith unto them, I go a-fishing. (JOHN 21:3.)

79. SATURDAY'S CHILDREN
   The disciples went away again unto their own home. (JOHN 20:10.)

80. THE VIGIL OF THE ANXIOUS HEART
   Mary stood without at the sepulchre weeping. (JOHN 20:11.)

81. THE VOICE WE RECOGNIZE
   "Mary." (JOHN 20:16.)

82. YESTERDAY'S TESTIMONY FOR TODAY'S FAITH
   Come, see the place where the Lord lay. (MATT. 28:6.)

83. TURNING OUR BACKS TO THE TOMB
   [Mary] turned round and saw Jesus. (JOHN 20:14 RSV.)

84. THE JOY OF THE MORNING
   Weeping may endure for a night, but joy cometh in the morning. (Ps. 30:15.)

85. DAWN OF NEW LIFE
   As it began to dawn. (MATT. 28:1.)

86. AND REMEMBER PETER
   Go . . . tell his disciples and Peter. (MARK 16:7.)

87. THE REVEALING HANDS
   Behold my hands. (LUKE 24:39.)

88. WHAT ROSE WITH CHRIST
   He has put an end to death and has brought Life and Immortality to light through the Good News. (II Tim. 1:10 Weymouth.)

89. THE STING OF DEATH IS BLUNTED
O Death, where is your sting? The victory is ours, thank God! He makes it ours by our Lord Jesus Christ. (I Cor. 15:55, 57 Moffatt.)

90. THE WORD FOR EASTER IS VICTORY
This is the victory that overcometh the world, even our faith. (I John 5:4.)

91. COMPELLING WITNESS
This Jesus hath God raised up, whereof we all are witnesses. (Acts 2:32.)

92. LIGHT FROM THE OPEN TOMB
The people that walked in darkness have seen a great light: they that dwell in the land of the shadow of death, upon them hath the light shined. (Isa. 9:2.)

93. JESUS AS TRAILMASTER
I will go before you into Galilee. (Matt 26:32.)

94. THE EASTER FAITH
Whosoever liveth and believeth in me shall never die. (John 11:26.)

95. THE FACT AND THE FAITH OF EASTER
If ye then be risen with Christ, seek those things which are above. (Col. 3:1.)

96. TOO GOOD TO BE TRUE!
While they yet believed not for joy, and wondered, he said unto them, Have ye here any meat? (Luke 24:41.)

97. THE GOSPEL OF THE RESURRECTION
Since we have become one with Him by sharing in His death, we shall also be one with Him by sharing in His resurrection. (Romans 6:5 Weymouth.)

98. HISTORY'S TURNSTILE
If Christ be not risen, then is our preaching vain, and your faith is also vain. (I Cor. 15:14.)

99. THE POWER OF HIS RESURRECTION

I would know him in the power of his resurrection and the fellowship of his sufferings, with my nature transformed to die as he died, to see if I too can attain the resurrection from the dead. . . . For all those of our number who are mature, this must be the point of view. (PHIL. 3:10, 15 Moffatt.)

100. RESPONSES TO THE RESURRECTION

When they heard of the resurrection of the dead, some mocked: and others said, We will hear thee again of this matter. (ACTS 17:32.)

101. SHARING CHRIST'S TRIUMPH

Now thanks be unto God, which always causeth us to triumph in Christ. (II COR. 2:14.)

102. HOPE-FILLED LIVES

Thank God, the God and Father of our Lord, Jesus Christ, that in his great mercy we men have been born again into a life full of hope, through Christ's rising from the dead! (I PET. 1:3 Phillips.)

103. EASTER'S AFTERGLOW

Because I live, ye shall live also. (JOHN 14:19.)

104. WHAT EASTER MANIFESTED

Christ . . . hath abolished death, and hath brought life and immortality to light through the gospel. (II TIM. 1:10.)

105. THE FAITH EASTER MAKES POSSIBLE

You will find trouble in the world—but, never lose heart, I have conquered the world! (JOHN 16:33 Phillips.)

106. RE-THINKING FAITH IN THE LIGHT OF EASTER

Then opened he their understanding. (LUKE 24:45.)

107. EASTER'S ENCOUNTER

He appeared unto the eleven . . . and upbraided them with their unbelief and hardness of heart, because they believed not them which had seen him after he was risen. (MARK 16:14.)

108. EASTER'S INVITATION

Christ also suffered for us, leaving us an example, that ye should follow his steps. (I Pet. 2:21.)

109. EASTER'S BENEDICTION UPON TWENTIETH-CENTURY CHRISTIANS

Blessed are they that have not seen, and yet have believed. (John 20:29.)

B. TOPICS FOR LENTEN SERIES

110. QUESTIONS ASKED OF JESUS DURING HIS LAST WEEK [1]

Art Thou a King? (John 18:37.)
What Shall Be the Sign of Thy Coming? (Matt. 24:3.)
Shall We Give Tribute to Caesar? (Matt. 22:17.)
Whose Wife in the Resurrection? (Matt. 22:28.)
Which Is the Great Commandment? (Matt. 22:35, 36.)
What Think Ye of Christ? (Matt. 22:41, 42.)
Art Thou the Son of God? (Matt. 26:63.)

111. HIS LAST WEEK [2]

Sunday: A Day of Triumph
Monday: A Day of Conquest
Tuesday: A Day of Controversy
Wednesday: A Day of Plotting
Thursday: A Day of Farewells
Friday: A Day of Tragedies
Saturday: A Day of Memories

112. THE QUESTION OF THE CROSS [3]

The Magnetism of the Cross
The Need for the Cross
The Reason for the Cross
The Substitute on the Cross
The Bitterness of the Cross
The Loneliness of the Cross

[1] Harold J. Ockenga, *Protestant Preaching in Lent.*
[2] J. W. G. Ward, *His Last Week.*
[3] Edward L. Keller, *The Question of the Cross.*

The Ignorance at the Cross
The Foolishness of the Cross
The Bearer of the Cross
The Verdict of the Cross

113. WHAT CRUCIFIED JESUS? [4]

Ecclesiasticism: The Pharisees
Privilege: The Sadducees
Nationalism: Judas
Opportunism: Pilate
Secularism: Herod
Militarism: The Soldiers
Acquiescence: The Public

114. GLORYING IN THE CROSS [5]

The Cross in the Law (HEB. 9:22.)
The Cross in the Prophets (LUKE 24:25-26.)
The Cross in the Psalms (LUKE 24:44.)
The Cross of Jesus (JOHN 19:25.)
The Cross in Christian Experience (MATT. 16:24.)
The Blood of the Cross (I JOHN 1:7.)
The Preaching of the Cross (I COR. 1:23.)

115. THEY CRUCIFIED AND CRUCIFY [6]

The Indifferent	The Greedy
The Unfair	The Traitorous
The Prejudiced	The Deserters
The Envious	The Cowardly
The Slanderers	The Crucified

116. CONFLICTS AT CALVARY [7]

Judas, Who Betrayed Him
Simon Peter, Who Lost His Nerve
Two Shrewd Politicians: Annas and Caiaphas
Herod, Who Bartered His Soul for Pleasure
Pilate, Who Tried to Shirk His Responsibility

[4] Harold Cooke Phillips, *In the Light of the Cross.*
[5] Harold J. Ockenga, *Protestant Preaching in Lent.*
[6] Edward L. Keller, *They Crucified and Crucify.*
[7] G. Ray Jordan, *Why the Cross?*

117. THE CLAIMS CHRIST MADE [8]

I Am the Bread of Life (JOHN 6:35.)
I Am the Light of the World (JOHN 8:12.)
Before Abraham Was, I Am (JOHN 8:58.)
I Am the Door (JOHN 10:9.)
I Am Come (JOHN 10:10.)
I Am the Good Shepherd (JOHN 10:11.)
Ye Call Me Master and Lord . . . For So I Am (JOHN 13:13.)
I Am the Way (JOHN 14:6.)
I Am . . . the Truth (JOHN 14:6.)
I Am . . . the Life (JOHN 14:6.)

118. NAILS OF THE CROSS [9]

The Nail of Pride (MARK 12:38-40.)
The Nail of Hatred (JOHN 15:23-25.)
The Nail of Envy (MATT. 27:18.)
The Nail of Indecision (MATT. 27:22.)
The Nail of Infidelity (MATT. 26:56.)
The Nail of Cruelty (ISA. 53:5.)

119. WORDS AT THE CROSS [10]

What the Governor Said (JOHN 19:22.)
What the Important People Said (MATT. 27:12-13.)
What the Spectators Said (Matt. 27:39-40, 47, 49.)
What the Church Leaders Said (MATT. 27:41-43.)
What the Condemned Criminals Said (LUKE 23:39-42.)
What the Army Officer Said (MARK 15:39.)
What the Crucified Said (MATT. 27:46; MARK 15:34; LUKE 23:34, 43, 46; JOHN 19:26-28, 30.)

120. THE INVINCIBLE CHRIST [11]

The Fascinating Christ (MARK 2:12.)
The Dawn-Bringing Christ (LUKE 1:78-79.)
The Preaching Christ (MARK 1:14-15.)
The Seeking, Saving Christ (LUKE 19:10.)
The All-Sufficient Christ (JOHN 6:67-68.)
The Reassuring Christ (LUKE 7:19, 22.)

[8] George Stewart, *Jesus Said "I Am."*
[9] J. R. Brokhoff.
[10] David A. MacLennan, *Resources for Sermon Preparation.*
[11] Massey Mott Heltzel, *The Invincible Christ.*

The Condescending Christ (LUKE 6:12, 17.)
The Serving Christ (JOHN 13:4.)
The Disturbing Christ (JOHN 11:56.)
The Risen Christ (JOHN 20:1.)
The Proclaimed Christ (ACTS 28:31.)
The Strengthening Christ (PHIL. 4:13.)
The Undefeated Christ (REV. 11:15.)

121. AND STILL HE SPEAKS [12]
The Word of Confirmation (JOHN 20:16.)
The Word of Salutation (JOHN 20:19.)
The Word of Faith (JOHN 20:29.)
The Word of Discipleship (JOHN 21:17.)
The Word for the World (MATT. 28:18-20.)
The Word from the Living Word (LUKE 24:32.)
The Word That Converts (ACTS 9:5.)
The Word to Be Preached (ACTS 4:33; I COR. 15:14-15.)
The Word Everlasting (MATT. 28:20; LUKE 24:50-53; HEB. 13:8.)

C. TOPICS FOR GOOD FRIDAY SERMONS

122. LESSONS THE CROSS TEACHES [13]
Forgiveness, Human and Divine (LUKE 23:24.)
What Death Could Mean (LUKE 23:39-43.)
Christ Taught Us to Care (JOHN 19:25-27.)
Black Despair and the Way Through (MATT. 27:46; LUKE 15:
33-39.)
Christ and Our Elemental Needs (JOHN 19:28-29.)
What Calvary Completed (JOHN 19:30.)
The Victory of the Cross (LUKE 23:44-49.)

123. LOVE SPEAKS FROM THE CROSS [14]
Love in Action (LUKE 23:24.)
Love Unconditional (LUKE 23:39-43.)
Love's Responsibilities (JOHN 19:25-27.)
Love's Extremity (MATT. 27:46; MARK 15:33-39.)
Love's Priorities (JOHN 19:28.)

[12] Edward L. R. Elson, *And Still He Speaks.*
[13] David A. MacLennan, *Resources for Sermon Preparation.*
[14] Leslie Badham, *Love Speaks from the Cross.*

Love's Consummation (JOHN 19:30.)
Love's Surrender (LUKE 23:44-49.)

124. FAITH FOR LIFE'S ENLARGEMENT
Faith Embraces Sinful Humanity (LUKE 23:24.)
Faith Rescues and Restores (LUKE 23:39-43.)
Faith and Love's Witness (JOHN 19:25-27.)
Faith Pierces the Darkness (MATT. 27:46; MARK 15:33-39.)
Faith That Overcomes (JOHN 19:28.)
Faith and Life's Mission (JOHN 19:30.)
Faith and Eternal Life (LUKE 23:44-49.)

125. SEVEN TIMELESS TESTIMONIES
Love Transcending Hate (LUKE 23:24.)
The Everlasting Mercy (LUKE 23:39-43.)
Strengthening Filial Piety (JOHN 19:25-27.)
When God Hides (MATT. 27:46; MARK 15:33-39.)
The Word Made Flesh (JOHN 19:28.)
Let Us Go On unto Perfection (JOHN 19:30.)
Divine Sonship (LUKE 23:44-49.)

126. CHRIST SPEAKS FROM CALVARY [15]
The Forgiving Christ (LUKE 23:24.)
The Compassionate Christ (LUKE 23:39-43.)
The Devoted Christ (JOHN 19:25-27.)
The Rejected Christ (MATT. 27:46; MARK 15:33-39.)
The Suffering Christ (JOHN 19:28.)
The Victorious Christ (JOHN 19:30.)
The Triumphant Christ (LUKE 23:44-49.)

127. SEVEN WORDS FOR MODERN MEN
A Message for Those Who Still Reject Him (LUKE 23:24.)
Encouragement for Prodigals (LUKE 23:39-43.)
Companionship for the Lonely (JOHN 19:25-27.)
For Those Who Would Call Quits (MATT. 27:46; MARK 15:33-39.)
For the Inasmuch Fellowship (JOHN 19:28-29.)
Finding Meaning for Our Lives (JOHN 19:30.)
Believing Where We Cannot Prove (LUKE 23:44-49.)

[15] Edward Jeffries Rees, *Christ Speaks from Calvary.*

IV. Galilee to Gethsemane

A. HIS FACE TOWARD JERUSALEM

128. EAGER DETERMINATION

We know the physical road Jesus traveled on this ever memorable journey. From beyond Jordan He was on His way to Jerusalem by way of Jericho. Our text tells us that as this company marched on their way up the steep ascent the disciples "were amazed, and they that followed were afraid." There was an eagerness about Jesus that was unusual even for Him. It was clearly evident that there was something in Jesus' mind, something on His heart, that wholly absorbed Him. They were all awed by Jesus' eagerness and determination.

The disciples thought they knew what was back of this far-away look, this eagerness, this haste. Jesus, they were hoping, was going to throw aside His temporary guise of lowliness and meekness and establish the long expected Messianic kingdom, a glorified, enlarged renewal of the old Davidic kingdom. But they were mistaken. It was not of this that Jesus was thinking; He was thinking of that new spiritual kingdom comprised of the elect of all races and nations. And he was looking straight ahead to Gethsemane, and Calvary, by which it was to be established. And He was beginning to feel the conflict and the pain even now. He had already begun to drink of the cup that very soon He was to drain to the last bitter drop.

Jesus saw all this. He saw the jealousy, the hatred, the intrigue, the treachery, the inhumanity and injustice with which He was to be treated. And yet He chose to go on and in going He exhibited an eagerness that might be compared with that of a bridegroom hastening to meet his bride on their wedding day. What is the explanation? Jesus did this because it was in the path of duty (John 4:34). But it was more; it was the call of love (John 13:1). When Jesus spoke of these things, His disciples tried to dissuade Him (Matt. 16:22). But in spite of all that Jesus saw at the end of the road, in spite of the dissuasive

43

powers of His disciples, He chose to go this way. Why? Because there was no other way. He came to redeem, to save the children of men. This was the price He had to pay to accomplish the purpose for which He had come into the world. And love made Jesus willing to pay the price, and to do it willingly, joyfully.

R. E. GOLLADAY

129. LOVE AND POWER

When Jesus set out for Jerusalem, he was facing directly into the place where all the pride, all the prejudice, all the power, all the smugness, bigotry, and materialistic cynicism, all the middle-class righteousness of his age was gathered together in concentrated form. The city represented the epitome of the sophistication and self-satisfaction of the age. He was deliberately placing himself and his gospel at the mercy of polite respectability as he advanced step by step toward the gates of the Holy City. He knew that his gospel of love was diametrically opposed to everything they thought and valued and did in Jerusalem. Of course they had been taught the power of love—Amos and Isaiah and Hosea had taught them. But they had never given it a wholehearted test. Like modern men, they tried it timidly with plenty of coercive *power* and force to back it up. He knew that he was throwing himself upon the wheel of destiny and the wheel would turn and slowly crush him. Love forever stands opposed to power. They are eternally incompatible.

RALPH S. BARBER

130. THE PACE QUICKENS

"Christ Hastening to His Cross," is the title of a famous sermon by Alexander Maclaren; and it is true to the fact. The pace of the journey quickened toward the end, as the hard road narrowed and the goal was near at hand. Over all the later parables there broods a deepening Shadow, a suggestion of swiftness, finality and separation; we hear of a "far country," of a "great gulf fixed," of a door closed and men knocking, of a hand at the window waving away guests who have come too late, of a Son cast out of a garden cruelly slain; of a sword that divides father and child, of a cup of fellowship refused, of a cup of forsakenness drained, of a bridegroom coming before the lights were lit. There was a timing in the life of Jesus—"my hour has not yet come," then, at the last, "my hour has come"—almost as if He worked on some timetable, walking toward an engagement which He must needs keep. He must "work while it is day, ere the night cometh," and have His work done; something He was sent to "finish," and dared not stop until He did.

JOSEPH FORT NEWTON

131. WE FOLLOW FROM AFAR

The gospel says of the ascent from Galilee to Jerusalem that Jesus went before his disciples. St. John says that, as the end drew near, Peter followed Jesus "afar off." That perhaps is the first impression which we get from the record. In the events as they unfold we are aware that Jesus goes before us, a long way before us, beyond anything we have ever experienced. He seems, as it were, to be so far ahead of us that we can hardly see him. What was true of Simon Peter is far more true of us; at best we follow afar off. We may not feel unfitted to have sat with the multitude on the hillside as he spoke the sermon on the mount. But to profess to have shared his passion is another matter. One is aware of what Nietzsche called "the pathos of distance" between ourselves and him. Sincerity requires that we do not claim too much for ourselves; that we admit from how far off we follow him.

WILLARD L. SPERRY

132. NEUTRALITY IMPOSSIBLE

Palm Sunday dramatized in unforgettable fashion this impossibility of neutrality on great issues. When we read that Jesus "stedfastly set his face to go to Jerusalem," we generally think of what that meant to Jesus, but today we are thinking of what it meant to Jerusalem. If only he had stayed away, what a relief! Why did they have to face that decision which split the city wide open, some welcoming him with hosannas and palm branches and some convinced he must be liqui-

45

dated? A disturbing nuisance Jesus was, coming thus to Jerusalem, and there is no use trying to keep ourselves out of that picture. Human nature being what it is, Christ is disturbing. We Christians commonly interpret him in terms of his loveliness; we call him glorious names; but he himself said he came to cast fire on the earth. Something incendiary about Jesus starts a conflagration wherever he appears. To our human nature he is upsetting. Why must we be haunted by his ideals so far above us, and made miserable by the necessity of choosing either for him or against? Would not life be easier if he had never come, so to challenge us with his demands?

HARRY EMERSON FOSDICK

133. CALL OF JERUSALEM

Every true life has its Jerusalem, to which it is always going up. A life cannot be really considered as having begun to live until that far-off city in which its destiny awaits it, where its work is to be done, where its problem is to be solved, begins to draw the life towards itself, and the life begins to know and own the summons. Very strange is this quality of our human nature which decrees that unless we feel a future before us we do not live completely in the present where we stand today. We have grown so used to it that we do not realize how strange it is. It seems to us to be necessary. But the lower natures, the beasts, do not seem to have anything like it. And we can easily picture to ourselves a human nature which might have been created so that it never should think about the future, but should get all its inspiration out of present things. But that is not our human nature. It always must look forward. The thing which it hopes to become is already a power and decides the thing it is.

And so every true life has its Jerusalem to which it is always going up. At first far off and dimly seen, laying but light hold upon our purpose and our will, then gradually taking us more and more into its power, compelling our study, directing the current of our thoughts, arranging our friendships for us, deciding for us what powers we shall bring out into use, deciding for us what we shall be: so every live man's Jerusalem, his sacred city, calls to him from the hill-top where it stands.

PHILLIPS BROOKS

134. INEXPRESSIBLE ANGUISH

The scene needs the genius of an artist rightly to describe it. Like a fairy spectacle, the Holy City lay peacefully beneath the afterglow of the setting sun. The tiny houses seemed to be nestling down for the night within the shelter of the walls. Familiar buildings could still be picked out, while surmounting the whole was the Temple, its walls still burnished by the tints of the sky. What moving memories centred in that sacred spot! The Master looked out from Olivet towards the city. There was a wistfulness in His eyes that haunts my heart to this day, for He saw the past, the present, and the future. What a story would those hills tell could they but speak! The tides of battle had swept about them like boisterous waves against a rock-strewn coast. David, the daring hero of Israel, had established his throne there, making Mount Zion his seat of power. Solomon, the splendid, had carried his father's schemes to completion, translating David's dreams into deeds. The royal palace, the imposing towers and fortifications, were surpassed, however, by the House of God. The finest materials procurable had been fashioned by skilled craftsmen from afar. The project had laid hold of the popular imagination to a surprising extent. And when at last, after years of arduous toil, the work was finished, the Temple was consecrated to God amid a blaze of magnificence. Then troubles came with the passing years. The city was besieged, the Temple ravaged and stripped by Nebuchadnezzar, and its rubble-strewn courts resounded with the desolate howl of jackals. Rebuilt by Zerubbabel, later desecrated by Antiochus Epiphanes and reconsecrated by Judas Maccabaeus, yet like some grim warrior, its turbulent history was written in the scars deep graven on its frame. Then Herod the Great, an Edomite time-server, had razed it to the ground, and rebuilt it both as a salve to his conscience and a means of securing the support of Jewish patriotism for his throne.

There it stood, the visible symbol of Judah's invisible God, and about it the peaceful homes of the city. Why then the look of inexpressible anguish in the Saviour's face? He saw what none other could see. The supersensitive soul has means of discerning the truth which others miss.

J. W. G. WARD

B. O JERUSALEM, JERUSALEM

135. AT JERUSALEM

Jerusalem, Jerusalem, who oft
His love had gathered thee beneath its wings
And thou wouldst not!—Love crucified aloft
On Calvary, enthroned the King of Kings.

KATHERINE LEE BATES

136. DIVINE COMPASSION

Picture Jerusalem on that Sunday morning, densely crowded for the Passover. Every house was full and every street was thronged; there were tens of thousands gathered there. And it was when our Lord, turning the crest of Olivet, saw before him that so crowded city, that like summer tempest came his tears. Tears for the one; tears for the twice ten thousand: how typical is that of the Redeemer! Never was there a compassion so discriminative, and never a compassion so inclusive. Our separate sorrows—he understands them all, and our hours of solitary anguish by the grave; but not less the problem of the crowd. There are men who are full of sympathy for personal sorrows, but have never heard the crying of the multitude. There are men who hear the crying of the multitude, but have never been broken-hearted at the tomb. Christ has room for all, and room for each. He loves the world with a divine compassion.

GEORGE H. MORRISON

137. DOUBLE FEELING

He reaches the holy city for which, like every devout Jew, He felt a patriot's love. It is cold to Him, God's Representative. With an assurance akin to that of the great prophet's He is confident of its doom. "O Jerusalem, Jerusalem!" is His heart-broken cry. His feelings are torn: on the one hand His conscience is in accord with God's judgment on an unresponsive people; on the other hand His heart grieves over countless little ones blindly fated to destruction. In 1877 Richard Green, the

48

historian of the English people, distressed by the public policy of the nation, wrote in a letter: "I love England dearly. But I love her too well to wish her triumphant if she fights against human right and human freedom. Pitt longed for her defeat in America, but it killed him when it came. I can understand that double feeling now." And it is a similar "double feeling" which we see in Jesus. He belongs to the unresponsive nation and is involved in its guilt and weeps over its approaching doom. He is God's Representative and must bring on the crisis in order that the kingdom may come. Yes, by forcing the issue He makes more sure of His own death, and that fills up the measure of His loved people's iniquity. If a "double feeling" in an English statesman's heart killed him, we gain some insight into a similar struggle in the anguished soul of Christ.

Henry Sloane Coffin

C. ENTRY IN TRIUMPH

138. LOVELY TO THE OUTWARD EYE

Lovely to the outward eye
Seemed Jerusalem to lie—
Yet 'twas there thou cam'st to die,
Jesus, Son of Mary.

Far-brought stones and marble rare
Made its towers and circuits fair,
Yet thy cross was waiting there,
Wearied Son of Mary.

Author Unknown

139. AROUND THE BROW OF OLIVET

Around the brow of Olivet
    In jubilant array,
The marching throng proceeds along
    Its gay, triumphal way.

They see the city, temple crowned,
  Where earnest people pray;
Expectant hearts give praise and sing,
  "Our King is come today!"

The voices once by silence bound,
  Long since by Him set free,
Now sing their alleluias forth
  In joyous ecstasy.
The eyes once closed in darkest night
  No longer grope their way;
Today they lead the festal march
  In fullest light of day.

The sick by palsied weakness held
  No longer prostrate lie,
They lift their waving palms aloft
  In glory to the sky.
"All hail!" they sing, "here comes your King,
  O Holy City, bright!
He comes to heal your broken hearts,
  His rule shall be your light."

ROLLAND W. SCHLOERB

140. EXPECTED MESSIAH

Judged in the light of any ordinary standards of regal splendor, military display, political campaigning, or effective advertising, it was a rather pathetic and anti-climactic affair. Jesus rode from Bethany upon a young ass, followed by his disciples, who were somewhat puzzled and anxious, and welcomed by a motley crowd of folk from the country districts who had come to Jerusalem for the Feast of the Passover and were hoping to find in him the expected Messiah. The procession started according to scheduled specifications, for there was a well-recognized prophecy that the Messianic King would come in such guise:

Tell ye the daughter of Zion,
Behold, thy King cometh unto thee,

50

Meek, and riding upon an ass,
And upon a colt the foal of an ass.

But it failed to end in Messianic style, for Jesus did not leap to the pinnacle of the temple, rend the clouds of heaven, summon a vast army of angels and archangels, expel the Romans from power, and compel them to bow their faces to the earth before his throne and acknowledge him to be sovereign. That was the orthodox program. That was what the Messiah was expected to do. Jesus did none of these things. He wept as he came in sight of the city, and prophesied its coming destruction. When he reached the temple, he "looked round about upon all things," the record says, and then returned to Bethany. The crowd melted away. It was a tame ending to their extravagant hopes.

Luther A. Weigle

141. VOCIFEROUS ENTHUSIASM

The triumphant entry into Jerusalem startles us by its apparent incongruity with the way of Jesus. It would surely be true to say that He preferred quiet, personal, and unobtrusive ways. It was a principle with Him to avoid the spectacular, and He kept a watchful eye on any rising tide of mass emotion. But His entry into Jerusalem *was* spectacular, and even sensational—and it was intended to be so. He arranged secretly beforehand with some unknown disciple for the loan of the animal. He accepted from the crowd, as though it were His due, demonstrations of loyalty which came near to worship. Hope and expectation swept like a tempest over the multitudes. The prophecy of Zechariah which St. Matthew recalls in this connexion cannot have been absent from the mind of Jesus, and it is worth while to continue it beyond the point at which the evangelist stopped. "Behold, thy King cometh unto thee: he is just, and having salvation; lowly, and riding upon an ass, even upon a colt the foal of an ass. And I will cut off the chariot from Ephraim, and the horse from Jerusalem, and the battle bow shall be cut off: and he shall speak peace unto the nations; and his dominion shall be from sea to sea, and from the River to the ends of the earth."

When Jesus rode into the city that day, silent among the shouting crowds, He knew how much and how little this vociferous enthusiasm meant. But He knew also that every habitable part of the earth had its representatives among the myriads gathered at Jerusalem that day, and all Jerusalem heard a message and were confronted with His claim before the night had come. The action of Jesus is consistent neither with humility nor good sense unless His mind had firm hold of a purpose which reached far back into the history of His people, and forward to a boundless reign of peace and blessedness. Nothing can save the Triumphal Entry from an intolerable theatricality if it was not the symbol of something at least as wonderful and transforming as the Christian Faith has declared Him to be. History has its comment to make. Now, after nineteen centuries, when He still has no Kingdom worthy of Him, and His people are so little like Him that the best of them are almost ashamed to claim His name, He yet has such a Kingdom and such a people as no one could have dreamed of then.

W. RUSSELL MALTBY

142. HE—THEY—WE

They hailed Him King as He passed by,
They strewed their garments in the road,
But they were set on earthly things,
And He on God.

They sang His praise for that He did,
But gave His message little thought;
They could not see that their souls' good
Was all He sought.

They could not understand why He,
With powers so vast at His command,
Should hesitate to claim their rights
And free the land.

Their own concerns and this world's hopes
Shut out the wonder of His news;
And we, with larger knowledge, still
His Way refuse.

He walks among us still, unseen,
And still points out the only way,
But we still follow others gods
And Him betray.

JOHN OXENHAM

143. ACTED PARABLE

The entrance into Jerusalem was an acted parable. It gave the faithful the sign they had been waiting for. It inaugurated the Master's final mission to his people and was a fitting prelude to the days of intense activity and emotion which were to follow. It focused the whole city's attention on Jesus, so that wherever he went during that closing week, crowds followed him, and his name was on every tongue. And, not least important, it flung down the gauntlet to his enemies. It defied them. Much they could endure, but this procession through the streets was intolerable. This fanatic and usurper must be put down finally. Jesus in that tumultuous hour was issuing a challenge. Every token of royal honor which he accepted that day gave point to the challenge, and every hosanna of the crowd drove it home. Let the powers of evil do their worst; he knew his power. He was the Lord's anointed. He was riding to the throne which God had given him. He was ready for the last campaign.

JAMES S. STEWART

144. LORD, WE WOULD FAIN

Lord, we would fain some little palm branch lay
    Upon Thy way;
But we have nothing fair enough or sweet
    For holy feet
To tread, nor dare our sin-stained garments fling
Upon the road where rides the righteous King.

Yet, Lord, our stubborn wills we first will break,
    If Thou wilt take;

53

And next our selfishness and then our pride,
    And what beside?
Our hearts, Lord, poor and fruitless though they be,
And quick to change and nothing worth to see.

Susan Coolidge

145. PALM SUNDAY

How scornfully the soldiers watched
That small procession go;
With what great pride and arrogance
Their legions wheeled to show
The might of Rome. But Caesars pass—
The court, the throne are dust,
The sword, the eagle-blazoned shield
And spear, alike, are rust.

Yet still through earth hosannas ring
In ever swelling tides,
And still across the centuries
The Galilean rides!

Leslie Savage Clark

146. ENTRY INTO A HEART

When He makes Triumphal Entry into a heart He redeems it from pettiness of self-expression and guides to the fulness of self-realization, bringing an abundance of life and peace. When he comes into a home, impatience gives way to loving kindness, love drives out tyranny and fear, and fretfulness is conquered by generosity. When He enters a city in triumph all arrogance, racial animosity, and class pride will be done away. It will mean emancipation and power and the healing of broken hearts; business will be done for the glory of God. . . . Men will say, "Today is the Kingdom of God come among us." It will come when He has made Triumphal Entry into human hearts, one by one.

Carl R. Simon

D. CHRIST AS KING

147. INTRUDER AND KING

Jesus came into Jerusalem . . . at once as an Intruder and a King. There were men along the streets who owed to Him the straightness of their limbs, the sight of their eyes, the clear, sane reason of their brains. They made the old streets ring with shouts of welcome. There were other men whom He had disappointed and defeated. He had trampled on their traditions, contradicted their doctrines, spoiled their trade. With muttered curses they saw Him go by in His triumph. What a confusion! The city was divided against itself. But through it all Jesus held on His way, claiming the town for His town because it was His Father's. Whether it owned His claim or spurned it, whether it welcomed Him or cursed Him, through the mixed tumult of its welcome and its curses He went on His way, claiming it all for His own. And so He claims our hearts. An Intruder and a King at once He seems to those hearts as He stands there on their threshold.

PHILLIPS BROOKS

148. FESTIVAL OF A PARADOX

Palm Sunday is the festival of a paradox, the paradox that lies at the very heart of the Christian faith. Jesus is the Messiah, and yet not the Messiah; nevertheless in a higher and final sense he is the Messiah— the one who was to come, and who came, and who is still to come. He was the Messiah of Jewish expectation, yet he was not, for he never fulfilled the nationalistic expectations of his people; and yet he was—and is—the Messiah in the sense that he more than fulfilled those expectations. He is the one whose coming the prophets had foretold; but the fulfillment so greatly exceeded the hope that we can only say, "He is the one whom the prophets dimly foresaw, interpreted and misinterpreted." As Robert Eisler described him in the Greek title which he chose for a largely perverse and mistaken historical study, Iesous Basileus *ou basileusas,* "Jesus the King who did not reign"— even so Christians have described him as the "uncrowned King." He was crowned, but it was with a crown of thorns, and his scepter was a reed. He did not reign; yet he does reign, he has reigned, he will reign, for ever and ever. For Jesus has reigned ever since his cruci-

55

fixion: as medieval artists and poets described him, borrowing the phrase from the Old Latin Psalter: *dominus regnavit a ligno*—"the Lord is reigning from the tree" (Ps. 96:10). That is how John understood the words, "If I be lifted up, I will draw all men to me" (John 12:32). That is how Paul understood the words, "He became obedient unto death, even death on a cross. Therefore God has highly exalted him and bestowed on him a name which is above every name, that at the name of Jesus every knee should bow, in heaven and on earth and under the earth" (Phil. 2:8-10).

Yet it is a paradox, which can be understood only by faith. And not only understood: for faith finds it the life-giving reality which expresses and explains all God's dealings with men, the clue to this all-encompassing mystery of our brief life here on earth, our alienation from God, our reconciliation to God, indeed our whole—and our only —salvation.

FREDERICK C. GRANT

149. A NEW SOVEREIGNTY

The sovereignty of Christ from the Cross is a new sovereignty. It has destroyed for ever the formula of material tyranny that might is right. It has put to shame the self-assertion of false heroism. It has surrounded with imperishable dignity the completeness of sacrifice. It has made clear to the pure of heart that the prerogative of authority is wider service. . . .

The sovereignty of Christ from the Cross is . . . also a universal sovereignty. It appeals in its principle to every man as based on love and not on fear. It claims with the attractiveness of blessing the service of every man. It speaks to every type of character. It leaves none desolate or uncared for or unoccupied. It brings to all the brotherhood of a divine origin, the equality of a common destiny, the freedom of self-surrender. . . .

The sovereignty of Christ from the Cross is again a present sovereignty. It is not for some distant future only, when there shall be no more sorrow and no more sin. It is for the transformation of the world which He has conquered. It corresponds with the circumstances of our troubled state. It is extended by the forces by which it was established. It is exercised still from the Cross, and through the Cross. It is directed to bring our common impulses under the conscious rule of a will harmonious with the will of God. . . .

Yet more the sovereignty of Christ from the Cross is a divine sovereignty. It answers to the very nature of God. God is love, and in love He reveals Himself as King. Christ upon the Cross establishes His own words in a way beyond the imagination of man: "He that hath seen me hath seen the Father." The sovereignty of Christ is in other words the victory of love, a victory won once for all by the Son of man and appropriated slowly by men as the years go on.

BROOKE FOSS WESTCOTT

150. KINGS CHOOSE THEIR SOLDIERS

Kings choose their soldiers from the strong and sound
And hurl them forth to battle at command,
Yet at the end, the whole wide world around,
Melts through Time's fingers, like the dropping sand.

But once a King, despised, forsaken, crowned
Only with thorns, chose in the face of loss,
Earth's poor, her weak, her outcast—gave them love
And sent them forth to conquer, in His name,
The world that crucified Him, and proclaim
His empire. Lo! pride's vanished thrones above,
Behold the enduring manner of the Cross.

PRISCILLA LEONARD

E. IN THE UPPER ROOM

151. ROOM OF MEMORIES

It is small wonder that this upper room has been a dearer place to Christendom than all the great cathedrals raised by subsequent ages to Jesus' honor. Its story was not finished when the Master rose from the table there and led his friends out to Gethsemane; it was not finished when the candles were extinguished that night and silence reigned again. For when after Calvary the brokenhearted, leaderless disciples sought a hiding place and refuge from the threatening mob, it was in this same upper room that they found it. This was the place which witnessed their hopeless mourning for the Master they had lost; and this was the place where that mourning was turned to bewildered, incredulous joy when Jesus came back to them through the closed and bolted door, and revealed himself risen and alive (John 20:19). Here, too, it is more than likely, they gathered again when he had ascended to his Father; and here the Spirit fell, flooding their souls with the glory of Pentecost and giving birth to the Christian Church (Acts 1:13, 2:1). If the tradition is correct which identifies this upper room with the house in Jerusalem to which Peter made his way on his escape from prison (Acts 12:12), we should be able to conclude that the "goodman of the house," who figures so mysteriously in the Gospel story (Mark 14:14), was none other than the husband of Mary, the mother of John Mark, the earliest evangelist. . . . The "certain young man" who according to Mark's Gospel was present in Gethsemane and escaped with difficulty when Jesus was arrested may have been Mark himself (Mark 14:51). We can imagine him helping his father and mother to prepare the upper room for Jesus and his friends, waiting outside the door while the Last Supper was celebrated that night, and then following the little group out to the garden on Olivet to see what was to happen. Be that as it may, this upper room of many memories will always draw and hold the hearts of Christ's people wherever the gospel is preached; and every time the bread of our Communion is broken and the wine poured out, we feel that we are meeting with Jesus there.

JAMES S. STEWART

152. MAUNDY THURSDAY

He lifts the round loaf in the darkening air,
Breaks the whole grief and gives to each a share.
The bread of heaven, transfigured, set on high,
Is the full moon that drowns the paschal sky,
Breaks its white blessing on the sleeping town.
—The loaf, the moon, the crown . . .

EDITH LOVEJOY PIERCE

58

153. THIS EUCHARISTIC FEAST

This eucharistic feast
Our every want supplies;
And still we by His death are blessed,
And share His sacrifice.

CHARLES WESLEY

154. LOVE AND SUFFERING

It is not only the simple, loving desire of Jesus to be as much in the company of His disciples as possible before the end came. This is the culmination of the whole work of the Redeemer, and the story is told that we may realize it to be so. The deeper explanation is found in this region. The time of the Master's baptism of fire is come, and as He had said before on looking forward to it: "How am I straightened until it be accomplished." It was the constraint of love to finish the work He had been given to do. The strange combination we find in the word "passion," as meaning both a great flame of love and a fierce flame of suffering, has never been so illustrated anywhere as in the Passion of our Lord. It was desire and anguish, sweet and bitter, love and suffering. When the hour was come and He sat down at the prepared feast, He said: "With desire I have desired to eat this Passover with you before I suffer."

HUGH BLACK

155. A LOAF OF BREAD, A JUG OF WINE, AND A TOWEL

The seed that's sown and harvested
Becomes this blesséd broken bread,

This blessed broken bread that's food
For lasting peace and brotherhood.

The tree that's trained to yield this wine
Will tell of sacrifice divine;

Of sacrifice My friends will make
Before the Day of God will break.

59

My friends will never overlook
What happened when this towel I took;

For all that bread and wine may say
A towel will tell eternally.

JOHNSTONE G. PATRICK

156. TEACHING BY SYMBOL

In that upper room where He kept the Passover with His disciples He showed each of them what a Paschal sacrifice should be. They had been quarrelling as to which should have the place nearest Himself. He taught them by a striking symbol that those nearest to Himself were the humblest in soul; He took a towel and girded Himself, and washed their feet. The evangelist prefaces his account of the deed by these words, "Knowing that He came from God and went to God." And many a preacher reading the words has pointed the moral thus, "Look how condescending Jesus was! Although He knew He was so far above these poor creatures both in His origin and in His destiny, He yet stooped beneath His conscious position!" That is not my reading of the passage, nor my moral from it. Where, think you, lies the connection in the thought of Jesus between washing the disciples' feet and remembering that He came from God and went to God? Is it not clearly this?—"My course has been humility all through—from beginning to end. When I came from God I came *down;* my mission was to surrender my own will. When I *go* to God I shall pass to Him through depths lower still—through the valley of the shadow of death. This act of service towards you is to me in keeping with all that is gone before and with all that is to follow." The clause is meant to *exclude* the idea of condescension, to show how *thorough* was the surrender of the true Paschal Lamb. The lamb of the Passover was offered only once a year; but the surrender of the will of Jesus had been made each morn and even.

GEORGE MATHESON

157. DEEPER MEANING

The ceremonial itself was not original. There had long been a similar Syrian custom in those days. When a man was to leave on a far journey, he gathered his friends together for a last pledge of affection. He gave them food with his own hands. It would be as his body to theirs in the time of absence. He also gave them wine. It would be as the blood of his life to their lives while they were parted. These things were to be a symbol of the fact that they would always be together even though separated.

In the hands of Jesus at the time of parting with his disciples, this simple ceremony took on a deep meaning. For Jesus knew that his work would end with his death unless his followers kept him at the focus of their memory and labors. It was no selfish desire just to be remembered that inspired this memorial. It was to be a living testimonial by the disciples of their own witness for him. Jesus was their leader, their friend, their Saviour. He knew that they would be victorious only as they kept their personal feeling for him alive and real. The institution of the Last Supper was to be a means to that end. He was tying them and their successors to himself forever.

CHARLES M. CROWE

158. MEDITATION FOR HOLY COMMUNION

At twilight hour the burdened Saviour came
With his disciples to the upper room.
The feast was spread, soft-lit by oil lamp's flame.
Each sensed the presence of impending doom.
"This is my body; take, and eat," he said;
"And drink the cup; my blood for you outpoured."
And as they ate and drank, their hearts he read
And found not one to him securely moored:
One would betray, another would deny,
And one escape from dark Gethsemane;
And one, unsure of self, said, "Is it I?"
The unpossessed of Christ thus never see!
Possess us, Lord, for otherwise we're lost;
Infuse thyself with us at Pentecost!

RUSSELL Q. CHILCOTE

159. ONE GREAT FELLOWSHIP

It began, this one great fellowship, in an upper room in the long ago when Jesus met with his disciples to keep the Passover. It was on the night when he was betrayed by Judas and just before his death on a cross. Who was the friend who provided this "upper room"? We do not know. He was one among many of the friends of Jesus who did a kindness for him but whose name we do not know. A fellowship was begun about a table on this tragic evening among the disciples of this Man of the centuries. This fellowship has increased and spread until now it covers the earth.

JESSE M. BADER

160. JESUS WHOSE LOT WITH US WAS CAST

Jesus, whose lot with us was cast,
Who saw it out, from first to last:
Patient and fearless, tender, true,
Carpenter, vagabond, felon, Jew:
Whose humorous eye took in each phase
Of full rich life this world displays,
Yet evermore kept fast in view
The far-off goal it leads us to:
Who, as your hour neared, did not fail—
The world's fate trembling in the scale—
With your half-hearted band to dine,
And chat across the bread and wine:
Then went out firm to face the end,
Alone, without a single friend:
Who felt, as your last words confessed,
Wrung from a proud unflinching breast
By hours of dull ignoble pain,
Your whole life's fight was fought in vain:
Would I could win and keep and feel
That heart of love, that spirit of steel.

AUTHOR UNKNOWN

F. IN THE GARDEN

161. MOST SACRED SCENE

Hardly dare we intrude on that most sacred scene in the life of our Lord when he and the Father communed together. And yet it is recorded here for us to meditate upon and to give some thought about it. It was the deepest experience in which our Lord engaged. It was on that occasion that he won the battle; he won it in the Garden of Gethsemane, not on the cross. The battle was already won before ever that cruel deed was executed.

I. W. GERNERT

162. JOHN'S PROPHECY

The eleven disciples, with Jesus at their head, descended from the city gates into the Valley of Jehoshaphat and crossed the brook Kidron to the Mount of Olives. Bishop Lightfoot tells us that all the blood drained from the Temple altars flowed into the Kidron. There is good reason to believe that at the time of the Passover, and perhaps even as Jesus and his disciples crossed the Kidron in the moonlight, the stream was running red. One wonders if John the Baptist's prophecy came into the mind of our Lord in that dread hour: "Behold the Lamb of God which taketh away the sin of the world!"

JOHN SUTHERLAND BONNELL

163. THE HIGH, HARD ROAD

The moment of crisis has come. The doom with which He has wrestled in the shadows is at hand. Shall He evade it or face it? The opportunity of choice is still His. He has but to turn and rush through the quiet protecting gloom of night, under trees, up over the Mount of Olives, down on the other side of its summit to Bethany, to reach His friends. There swift assistance would be His for the asking. He could speed down the Jericho Road to the Jordan Valley and then travel quickly northward to Galilee. There His friends would protect Him. There He could hide, if need be, in the labyrinth of caves in the Valley of Doves, between Nazareth and Capernaum, near to His loved Galilee. There He would be safe. The way of escape is wide open. Life and the freedom to continue His ministry could be His if only He would run away. But the consecration made at the high altar of His prayer holds Him. He chooses to face the high, hard road that leads Him to a cross.

Lynn James Radcliffe

164. GREATEST OF LESSONS

The picture of Gethsemane is by universal consent one of the most moving pictures of human history. The prophets and Psalmists of old Israel and the supreme poet of the Book of Job had given perhaps more powerful and constant expression than is to be found anywhere else in literature to the horror of the righteous soul at the spectacle of triumphant evil, and the bewildered agony of the believing mind at the seeming indifference of God. All this horror and agony are here seen possessing the soul of Jesus. His spirit is free from the sense of sin. He has wholly sought the Father's will. He has served to the uttermost for the needs of men. Now he looks around and finds himself deserted and alone. He looks forward and sees what is to happen. Those in whose hands he is are moving wholly under the power of the Evil One. All that he must bear—the death he must die—is a hideous anomaly. So he pleads in agony of soul against the monstrous horror of it all, while at the same time his human will holds on its allotted way in flawless obedience. "Father, if it be possible, let this cup pass from me. Nevertheless, not my will, but thine be done." Surely the author of the Epistle to the Hebrews is right when he finds the supreme moment of spiritual strain and trial, not on the Cross, but in Gethsemane. Anticipation is often a greater strain than actual endurance. So it was when Jesus "offered up strong crying and tears unto Him that was able to save him from death, and having been heard for his godly fear, though he was a Son yet learned obedience (the greatest of all lessons) from the things that he suffered." Three times he prayed in agony and three times he found his most intimate friends asleep. But the struggle is over. He stands now composed, and so remains to the end.

Charles Gore

165. EDEN AND GETHSEMANE

He who walks a garden path
Treads holy ground,
For there were man's high hopes destroyed—
And found.

LESLIE SAVAGE CLARK

166. PRAYER WAS HIS HABIT

If one says that in the crisis of his last week in Jerusalem Jesus turned
to prayer in the Garden of Gethsemane, the answer is that plainly he
did not turn to it as an unaccustomed, emergency measure. Note the
brevity of his praying! He faced an emergency indeed; there was no
time for long supplication; it was too late for him to have broken
an untraveled path to the presence of the Father. He could pray so
briefly yet so powerfully in the garden because prayer had been his
habit before. When, therefore, the ambush was sprung and the terrific
crisis was on him, his feet followed a familiar path and his words were
few: "Not my will, but thine, be done." What reorientation of life
a moment of prayer can work in one to whom it is habitual! But if
one is to have this experience when he critically needs it, he must
have known it *before.*

HARRY EMERSON FOSDICK

167. UNDERSTANDING GETHSEMANE

Gethsemane's reality, undoubtedly, has suffered much at the hands
of both the artist and the theologian. The artist has dared to invest
the scene with beauty when sorrow and horror should have been written
large over all. The theologian has generally supplied elaborate explanations and interpretations when the simple narrative is so much more
compelling and convincing than anything that can be said about it.
There is a better way than these for understanding Gethsemane, dark
though its shadows may be. Let men hate sin as He hated it, let
them love men as He loved them, let them dare to walk by faith even
into the outer darkness for the sake of good to others. In these ex-

periences Gethsemane shall be understood; its dark shadows shall flee away and, standing there, the eager soul shall see God waiting with outstretched hands of love.

GERHARD E. LENSKI

168. *FROM* GETHSEMANE

All those who journey, soon or late,
Must pass within the garden gate;
Must kneel alone in darkness there,
And battle with some fierce despair.
God pity those who cannot say,
"Not mine, but thine," who only pray,
"Let this cup pass," and cannot see
The *purpose* in Gethsemane.

ELLA WHEELER WILCOX

V. Personalities of the Passion

A. PETER

169. FRIEND WHO DENIES

Of all the men who had a part in wounding and killing Jesus, Peter least expected to. He was so sure that he never would. But that very self-assurance forewarned Jesus of what could be expected of him. It is a well-known psychological truth that men brag most about the virtues which they do not possess, and condemn most harshly in others the vices which flourish within their own hearts. The bully is the coward, and "the bravest are the tenderest."

Peter had been one of the three disciples closest to Jesus. He really loved the Lord. He did not want to hurt him. But he did hurt him. It always hurts to be denied by a trusted friend. Surely the jeers and sneers of passers-by did not wound Jesus so deeply as did the denial of Peter, anticipated though it was.

In our own day, those who can hurt Jesus most are not the skeptics and the scoffers, but professing Christians. His cause today is most seriously threatened not by those who announce themselves hostile to it, but by those who claim allegiance to it. His church is weakened most not by those without its ranks but by those within. Since the time of Peter, the problem of Christianity has not been that of gaining adherents, but rather that of holding the devotion and loyalty of those who nominally accept it. It is relatively easy to increase the membership of any church, but it is infinitely harder to keep that membership loyal and active.

TALMAGE C. JOHNSON

170. THE LORD'S GLANCE

We are apt to speak depreciatively of Peter's denial, and appreciatively of his later life. But there is one thing we do not sufficiently mark—

that a glance was enough for him. There is scarcely one in a million for whom, in those circumstances, a glance would be enough. As people now are, they would probably, every one of them, have thought themselves exceedingly lucky if they had, to their great self-satisfaction, *prudently* left the Master in the lurch. And if he had fixed his glance on them, every one of them would have complacently thought, I was prudent enough to seem as if I had not noticed anything.

SØREN KIERKEGAARD

171. SPIRITUAL TRIUMPH

It is altogether likely that the one thing which kept Simon Peter from making the tragic mistake of Judas Iscariot is the look which Jesus gave him, following Simon's denial of his Lord. Although we have only a brief record of the incident, we know enough about Jesus to be sure that he did not look at Simon in anger. His face must have shown disappointment—the keenest kind of pain—but we can also be certain that the countenance of Christ portrayed forgiveness, belief in this disciple, and love for him. It seems quite clear that this was the turning point for Simon Peter. Instead of being defeated by remorse, he won the spiritual triumph that comes from repentance.

G. RAY JORDAN

172. PRESSING FORWARD

Peter did not spend the balance of his days with eyes red from weeping, and mind shattered with worrying, but from the very day of Pentecost, Peter was simply irresistible in his extension of the gospel. Working, praying, preaching, teaching—looking not behind except to gather new impetus from the memory of his Master's life, but pressing forward continually, he became indeed the rock upon which the church was to find a firm foundation—safe and sure. And if Peter ever did look back to his act of perfidy it must have been in the spirit which inspired Tennyson to say, "I hold it truth with him who sings, To one clear harp in diverse tones, That men may rise on steppingstones, Of their dead selves to higher things!"

LLOYD C. DOUGLAS

173. AS PETER LOVED

And immediately Jesus stretched for his
hand and caught him. MATTHEW 14:31.

As Peter loved I love, and in his fashion:
With boastful promises and bursts of passion;
Then anxious waverings and hot denials,
And faith that drowns amid a sea of trials.
Yet strong beyond my fitful love I see
His love forever reaching out to me.

JEAN HOGAN DUDLEY

B. JUDAS

174. MAN OF PROMISE

The Master's eye, accustomed to read all kinds of men, detected in
Judas the makings of a real apostle; here was a man who had it in
him to do splendid service for the Kingdom. Sometimes, indeed, it has
been suggested that Jesus gave Judas a place near himself simply because it was necessary for God's predestined plans that there should
be a traitor in the disciple band. It cannot be too strongly insisted that
any such theory is both absurd and irreligious. It turns predestination
into fatalism. It is a slander on providence and on God's ordering of
the world. It degrades the sacred narrative to the level of solemn play
acting. No, Jesus called Judas to be a disciple for the same reason for
which he called the other eleven. He saw in him a man of noble promise and boundless possibilities. No doubt he saw other things as well—
moral contradictions jostling one another in the man's secret soul,
strange conflicts of light and darkness, courage and cowardice, self-
surrender and self-love. But that simply meant that he was a man of
human passions, and it was out of such materials that Jesus fashioned
his saints. He hoped to do it here. Judas, when he first became a disciple, was a potential man of God.

JAMES S. STEWART

69

175. DISILLUSIONMENT AND DISAPPOINTMENT

There was no doubt [of] jealousy and avarice in Judas—but neither one in my judgment explains his act. It is true that were we to confine ourselves to the direct evidence of the Gospels we could reach no other conclusion. There is, however, indirect evidence for the position, usually attributed to Thomas De Quincey and now shared by many, that Judas was a disillusioned nationalist. I share the view of those New Testament scholars and writers who believe that Judas betrayed Jesus because he was a disillusioned and disappointed man. The kingdom as he envisioned it was the Davidic kingdom restored in all its glory, with Israel possessor of the power and prestige. It was a nationalistic kingdom. Jesus on the contrary visualized a universal kingdom. But this concept Judas could not understand.

One can imagine this proud Judean, in whose heart glowed the hope of Israel's restoration, saying to himself during the last week of Jesus' earthly life: "Why did he on his triumphant entry refuse the proffered crown? What does he mean by 'Blessed are the meek'? Whoever heard of a meek king? What can he mean when he speaks of Messiah going to Jerusalem to suffer and die? What a fine climax this is for the long-looked-for deliverer of our nation! What does he mean when he says, 'Love your enemies,' when those enemies have invaded your capital city? 'Pray for them that despitefully use you,' when such people stalk your streets? Maybe I do not understand him. I must find out. And the way for me to find out is to put him in a position where he will have to act. I will arrange it so that this man who claims to represent and possess the power of God will be brought face to face with earthly power. Maybe then he will summon his legions of angels to deliver him." His betrayal was an attempt to force Jesus' hand. His mind was torn between "disappointment and tempestuous hope." Even if his motives may not have been quite so sinister as we have supposed, still I believe with Henry Sloane Coffin that in forcing Jesus to declare himself, he "did it vindictively, not affectionately." Sholem Asch in *The Nazarene* has Jesus say to Judas: "Judah, thy heart is restless, it is like a lost ship in a stormy sea. Why canst thou not find rest, like my other disciples?" And Judas replies: "Rabbi, perform now one of thy wonders and strengthen my faith in thee." But he performed no wonder. Peter drew his sword—the weapon Israel's deliverer was expected to use—and Jesus said: "Put up . . . thy

sword; . . . they that take the sword shall perish with the sword." As
if to say, "This kingdom of mine uses other weapons."

HAROLD C. PHILLIPS

176. STILL AS OF OLD

Still as of old men by themselves are priced—
For thirty pieces Judas sold himself, not Christ.

HESTER H. CHOLMONDELEY

177. HIDDEN MOTIVES

The world has agreed to regard Judas as the chief of sinners; but, in
so judging, it has exceeded its prerogative. Man is not competent to
judge his brother. The master passion of Judas was a base one; Dante
may be right in considering treachery the worst of crimes; and the
supreme excellence of Christ affixes an unparalleled stigma to the
injury inflicted on Him. But the motives of action are too hidden, and
the history of every deed is too complicated, to justify us in saying
who is the worst of men. . . .

Two things it is our duty to do in regard to Judas: first, not so to
palliate his sin as to blunt the healthy, natural abhorrence of it; and,
secondly, not to think of him as a sinner apart and alone, with a nature
so different from our own that to us he can be no example. But, for the
rest, there is only one verdict which is at once righteous, dignified and
safe; and it is contained in the declaration of St. Peter, that he "went
to his own place."

JAMES STALKER

178. WHAT JUDAS BETRAYED

More important than the question *why* Judas was a traitor is the question *what* he betrayed. The rulers wanted a "good opportunity" to
arrest Jesus. No place could have been better for this purpose than the
enclosure of Gethsemane, and no time so opportune as the night of
the Passover, when all the people who might make a tumult were

celebrating in their several houses the solemn supper, or were sleeping like the Apostles. Judas could lead them to this place. But this surely was not the most indispensable service he could render the high priests, who by their secret agents would have been able to discover where Jesus passed the night. What they did not know, and what only one of the Twelve could betray to them, was Jesus' claim to be the Christ. The betrayal by Judas of this secret accounts for the fact that the High Priest, when he was able to produce no witnesses, put this question to Jesus.

WALTER LOWRIE

179. MISSING EASTER

The older I grow the more I ponder Judas Iscariot. He came so near to *not* betraying Jesus. He was a loyal disciple. It took courage to join that little band, and Judas had it. Then doubts began. What kind of Messiah was this who refused violent revolution and talked about loving one's enemies? Was not this idealistic Jesus letting them down? So the doubts grew, until in an explosive hour—oh, fifty-one votes against forty-nine—Judas sold his Lord. He came so near *not* doing it, that when he saw what he had done he hanged himself in shame. Ah, Judas, if you had only doubted your doubts enough to wait until Easter, until Pentecost, until Paul came, you would not be the supreme traitor of the centuries. You stood in the presence of divine greatness, and you disbelieved.

HARRY EMERSON FOSDICK

C. ANNAS AND CAIAPHAS

180. CONTRASTING PRINCIPLES

Two entirely different principles of life are personified in the meeting of Jesus and Annas. How vividly they are portrayed! Here was an old man who thought of everything and everybody in terms of how he could use them. His aims and purposes had to do with material things. Though he practiced his cunning under the guise of religion, he did not believe in the reality of the unseen. His life was not guided by high religious ideals. Seventy-year-old Annas was convinced that only place and power and prestige counted. Possessions were worth more than a sense of honor.

Now he was looking upon a man whose whole life was guided by the everlasting principles of right. Here was Jesus facing him, who had said that a man should be willing to give up every material possession, if need be, in order to keep his conscience clear. Annas did not know how to do anything "out in the open." Jesus was never ashamed of anything he did. He was willing for everything in the records of his life to be read by everybody. Jesus was clear in his thinking, honest in his purposes and plans, and always went straight as an arrow toward his goal of goodness. He was uncompromisingly devoted to truth and love. Annas had lived in secret conference rooms and had used people who were willing to do what he told them in order to gain some little recognition or economic security.

G. Ray Jordan

181. CAIAPHAS WROTE THE PLOT

Who is primarily responsible for the crucifixion of Christ? Not Pilate, for when Christ was brought to him on Friday morning the sentence had been pronounced, "He is guilty of death" (Matt. 26:66), and Christ Himself said to Pilate, "He that delivered me unto thee hath the greater sin" (John 19:11). Not Judas, for when he asked the priests, "What will you give me, and I will deliver him unto you?" (Matt. 26:15) the plans for the execution had long been made. Not the mob, for it had sung "Hosanna" in sincere joy on Sunday and was echoing the desires of only a few leaders when it screamed those monstrous two words, "Crucify Him!" Not the soldiers, for they were under orders when they nailed Christ to the cross. All had a part in the guilt of the crucifixion; no one in all humanity is innocent of the blood of that just Man. But the chief responsibility for the crucifixion of Christ falls on him who plotted it. Who wrote the plot? It was a collaboration, of course, but one man was the leader.

Armin C. Oldsen

73

182. HIS CHARACTER

Caiaphas stands out so clearly upon the page of Scripture that we cannot mistake his character. His unflinching and implacable enmity imprinted itself indelibly on the minds of the Apostles. In scene after scene he is distinctively drawn. We see him in the Council with the note of scorn in his speech, his easy mastery of the moods and fears of men, his bold, definite counsel. We see him in the interview with Jesus, rending his robes with histrionic fervour, in a finely simulated horror at the blasphemy of Christ. We see him playing his game with Pilate, and using that able Roman as his tool. We see him when Judas, torn with relentless remorse, bursts into the Council Chamber, turning away from the conscience-stricken man, dismissing the poor fool from his presence with a phrase. We see him, unchanged, when Peter and John stand before him, and he charges them to hold their peace. Who is this resolute, defiant, merciless man? He is the high priest of God—the holder of the holiest office in Judaism. What is he? An astute and unscrupulous diplomatist; a wily manager of men; a master of assemblies with a fitting gift of speech; a conceiver of bold and daring policies in the hour when others waver, and a man of unflinching will in carrying them out. How shall we describe this man of the holy office, and the crafty speech, and the diplomatic skill, in a single word? In one word, he is an ecclesiastic—the type of all that long succession of men who have laid heavy burdens on every church, and often thwarted the purpose of God.

W. M. Clow

D. HEROD

183. SOUL OF A WORLDLING

He was a man of good birth, although, like many other such men, with a dubious ancestry, if you go back far enough. He was a handsome man, of graceful address, with a naturally sunny temper, fond of gay trappings and of dainty living, with the constant tendency of such men to give way to appetite. He had no strength of mind or will. His one strength was the fury of a profligate's passions, a strength which many weak men share with the brutes, and, like so many of these men, he had a fatal fascination for women. But he was more than a splendid animal. He was a man of artistic temperament, with a fine taste in music and a discerning eye for colour. He was full of political ambitions and eager for place and title. He did not live aloof from his time, and he felt the better impulses which were moving and stirring men in Galilee. He had his code of honour, and shrunk from breaking his word; he had his hours of tender feeling and his moments of compunction. He had his religious opinions, and had naturally become a Sadducee, and he could break a lance in a theological discussion. But only lift your eyes from the pleasant face of this high-placed, polished-spoken, passion-driven, and superstitious man, and look into the spiritual world; only think of some face radiant with the sheen of holiness; only recall some voice pleading with God in well-accustomed prayer; only think of Jesus and His grace, only whisper this one word, God, to your own heart, and then look at Herod, and you see right past his wine-flushed skin into the soul of him, and you see him to be in one word—a worldling. The story of Herod in the Gospel page is the history of the soul of a worldling.

W. M. CLOW

184. HE WAS PAST FEELING

Herod displayed a man of the world's versatility in asking Him "many questions"—one wonders what they were. He was clever and was pleased to display his knowledge of religious fine points before his companions and before the priests. It was a chance to impress them. But Herod could make nothing of Jesus. And Jesus could make nothing of Herod. He had borne witness to his Messiahship before Caiaphas and the Sanhedrin; He had admitted His kingship to Pontius Pilate; but He had not a syllable to utter to Antipas. The tetrarch had heard of Him as a wonderworker and craved the chance to see Him do something startling. But Jesus' mighty works are not tricks to entertain and astonish. Herod had a conscience; could not Jesus appeal to that with some piercing story such as Nathan told adulterous David? Did the Saviour ever confront a needier sinner? But He had not a word for him.

Herod was apparently "past feeling," and Jesus gave him up. This clownish roysterer and his cronies could think of nothing to do with their disappointing Prisoner but tog Him out in mock finery and make game of Him. Fancy the mind of Jesus while this went on! It cost Pilate some struggle to condemn Him; but when He was sent away from the tetrarch's palace, Herod had been laughing at Him as a buffoon, and was now smiling at his own shrewdness in outwitting the governor, and handing his awkward case back to him.

HENRY SLOANE COFFIN

E. PILATE

185. QUESTION OF TRUTH

Jesus and Pilate stood contrasted in most of life's externals—Jew and Roman, prisoner and governor, carpenter and man of the world. But deeper than any of these is the inner contrast which their words revealed. Jesus has lived and is about to die for the truth; Pilate sneeringly questions whether there be any truth.

LUTHER A. WEIGLE

186. HE WAS DEAD TO TRUTH

This is the last desperate attempt of a man who had majored in evasiveness all his life to escape responsibility. He had chased with the dogs and run with the hares for so long that he thought he could outsmart everybody, including the King of truth. Until he was brought face to face with Jesus, he had considered himself an expert in the fine and difficult art of carrying water on both shoulders. Now at his wit's end, he resorted to theatrics, washing his hands in full view of the public. His grand strategy of sending Jesus to Herod having ended in complete failure, he calls for the basin of evasion and irresponsibility, "I am innocent of this righteous man's blood; see to it yourselves."

This pathetic and manifestly absurd plea of innocence means that Pilate was dead long before his frame collapsed. He was dead to truth, but alive to cynicism. His conscience had expired long ago, and he heard only the call of opportunism. On the altar of political expediency he had sacrificed the costly and precious gift of integrity, and as a substitute he had accepted the burnt-out ashes of personal ambition to serve and improve himself only. He had lived with falsehood for so long that he believed and followed and loved lying and treachery. "Cowards such as he die many deaths, the valiant but once," and even so their works do follow them.

G. ERIK HAGG

187. PERTINENT QUESTION

Pontius Pilate in an uncomfortable moment of perplexity, enquired of the crowd that sought Jesus' life: "What, then, will ye do with Jesus?" This query seems to echo through the centuries. Of course, any individual who stolidly refuses to recognize the question can continue to live his whole life without giving it his attention; but only as a pensioner upon the people who do recognize it as worthy of a reply.

LLOYD C. DOUGLAS

188. BEFORE PILATE

What utter loneliness He knew
When His own race could plot
His death; when those He healed had fled,
Their benefits forgot;
And thrice a loved disciple vowed,
"I know Him not!"

LESLIE SAVAGE CLARK

F. SIMON OF CYRENE

189. DAY OF BLESSEDNESS

This Simon, the Cyrenian, was just a plain man, coming into town on his own business, and meeting at the gate this turbulent group surging out toward the place of crucifixion, with the malefactor in their midst. Suddenly Simon finds himself turned about in his own journey, swept back by the crowd with the cross of another man on his shoulder,

77

and the humiliation forced upon him which there seemed no reason for him to bear. . . . And yet, how certain it is that this man of Cyrene came to look back on this interruption of his journey as the one thing he would not have missed. When others were remembering the wonderful career of Jesus, how often he must have said: "Yes, but I once had the unapproached privilege of bearing his cross for him. . . . It seemed a grievous burden, but it has become my crowning joy. I did not know then, but I know now, that my day of humiliation was my day of highest blessedness."

FRANCIS GREENWOOD PEABODY

190. I THINK OF THE CYRENIAN

I think of the Cyrenian
Who crossed the city-gate,
When forth the stream was pouring
That bore thy cruel fate.

I ponder what within him
The thoughts that woke that day
As his unchosen burden
He bore that unsought way.

Yet, tempted he as we are!
O Lord, was thy cross mine?
Am I, like Simon, bearing
A burden that is thine?

Thou must have looked on Simon;
Turn, Lord, and look on me
Till I shall see and follow
And bear thy cross for Thee.

HARRIET WARE HALL

191. INESCAPABLE BURDEN

Nobody can ever do just that service for Christ again. That glory none can share with Simon. But I am thinking that in one way or another we all find ourselves sooner or later in the grip of some irking compulsion against which we are disposed to rebel. Life, like some old Roman legionary, drafts us for a disagreeable service, lays upon us some inescapable burden, brings us face to face with some grim necessity. We are going our way, attending to our own affairs, when an arresting hand is laid upon us and we find ourselves thrown out of our course, our plans broken, our intention twisted out of its original design. . . . But if we get hold of the right end of these compulsions we may win the enrichment and blessing which they carry at their heart.

WILLIAM ORLANDO CARRINGTON

192. ON THE ROAD TO SKULL HILL

In Nazareth, I think, his home;
  His name? I never knew.
He was an enemy of Rome;
  Besides, he was a Jew.

The soldiers, when they saw him fall,
  Beckoned me, but I ran;
Then, seeing I was out of call,
  Took a Cyrenian.

Skull Hill looks hot . . . this road's a glare . . .
  How very long the way!
The cross I would not help him bear
  I bear alone today.

ELLEN GLINES

G. BARABBAS

193. THE CHOICE BEFORE THEM

One of the most interesting variant readings in the entire New Testament is found in Origen and in the Jerusalem and Syriac cursive manuscripts where the full name of Barabbas is given—"Jesus Barabbas." "Jesus," or "Joshua," was a relatively common Hebrew name, meaning deliverer or savior. It is perfectly evident why the variant reading was not generally accepted. According to the rules of textual criticism, the difficult readings are probably correct. This gives ground for believing that the crowd was faced with an interesting choice, "Will you have *Jesus Barabbas* or *Jesus the Christ?*"

HILLYER H. STRATON

194. DRAMATIC MOMENT

As the Evangelists tell us the story of Barabbas, they focus our attention on one moment of his life. It is that dramatic moment in which Jesus and Barabbas pass out of Pilate's presence together, which is to them so full of pathetic suggestions. The first thought in their minds, as in the mind of every one who knows the story, is the *startling and amazing contrast of their fate.* A man of genius and skill, in our generation, George Tinworth, has worked out, in terra-cotta, the scene at this dramatic climax, with a discerning spiritual insight. From one door, passing before Pilate's judgment-seat, there issues Barabbas, smiling in exultation. The soldiers grasp him by the hand in rude congratulations. His friends seize him in transports of joy. The mob hails him with acclamation. By the other door, held by the hard grip of the callous soldiers, seeing no kindly face looking towards him, confronted by the relentless hate of the infuriated multitude, there issues Jesus. In all the crowd there is only one discerning, pitying heart. The artist has placed, not very far from Christ's door, a woman with a little child in her arms, and she turns on Jesus as He passes her wondering and compassionate eyes. The woman with the child, alone of all the throng, sees whose is the victory and the unfading glory. That is a master touch. To this day men walk our streets, and sit in our high places, with the triumphant pride of Barabbas, and neither they themselves nor others know how completely they have failed. We seldom see with the eyes of the understanding, where true failure and true success lie.

W. M. CLOW

195. BARABBAS SPEAKS

I heard a man explaining
(they said his name was Paul)

how Jesus, on that fateful day,
had died to save us all.

I found it hard to follow
His fine-spun theory,
but I am very, very sure
He died that day for me.

EDWIN McNEILL POTEAT

196. BARABBAS SPEAKS

An hour till crockcrow and the inn asleep,
Yet I who lately knew
A guard and chains sit here alone,
And find no zest in brew,
Or tale, or song—remembering
One whom—for me—they slew.

LESLIE SAVAGE CLARK

H. THE CROWDS

197. PASSIVE TOLERANCE

It is difficult to believe that the common people tried of set purpose
to crucify Jesus. The people were always the friends of Jesus. The
evidence of the Gospels seems to show that he was tried, condemned,
and put to death, not by the nation as a whole, but by the priestly
and official classes within the nation. No doubt a certain section of
the people was involved in this crime. But they were not the big-
hearted, well-meaning, and kindly-disposed multitude. The crowd
which helped to precipitate this miscarriage of justice was only a
small section of the children of his generation. They were not the religious pilgrims to Jerusalem, but the priest-ridden and the priest-paid
canaille from the slums of the city. The authentic democracy who
adored Christ and whom he loved and trusted—the less intolerant Jews
of the Dispersion and the unsophisticated peasants of Judaea and Galilee—were not and could not have been parties to this crime. It is putting

too great a strain on our credulity to ask us to believe that the people who strewed the road to the Holy City with palm branches and shouted, "Hosanna!" were the same people as those who within a few measurable hours cried out, "Crucify him!"

Nonetheless, the democracy of Jerusalem cannot be absolved from complicity in the death of Jesus. They may not actively have compassed his death, but they passively tolerated it. At least they took no steps to prevent it. They were inactive when they should have been resolutely purposeful. They remained silent when they should have been vocal. They stayed indoors when they should have been abroad in force, making their influence felt. They were preoccupied, cautious, or afraid when the situation demanded alertness, courage, and decision. In the restrained language of Luke "they stood looking on" when they ought, by every compulsion of their better nature, to have resisted this monstrous wrong to the shedding of blood.

Robert Menzies

198. PALM SUNDAY AND MONDAY

They pluck their palm branches and hail Him as King,
  Early on Sunday;
They spread out their garments; hosannas they sing,
  Early on Sunday.

But where is the noise of their hurrying feet,
  The crown they would offer, the sceptre, the seat?
Their King wanders hungry, forgot in the street,
  Early on Monday.

Edwin McNeill Poteat

199. SPELL OF HYSTERIA

"And their voices prevailed." It was not their reason, their logic, their good sense, or the evidence in the case! The entire city fell under the terrible spell of hysteria. It was the noise they made which turned the head of Pilate.

Let us not be too hard on Pilate. Voices are very terrible weapons, against which there is sometimes very little defense. For that reason every Christian is under a sober responsibility to be careful about the cause to which he lends his voice.

Roy L. Smith

200. TRANSFORMING POWER

The crucifixion of Jesus took place before crowds. To most of these spectators it had no religious meaning whatsoever. It was the execution of a Galilean teacher, whom the authorities had found troublesome and were putting out of the way. These onlookers may have pitied Him as the unfortunate victim of circumstances, or they may have approved of His execution. But in them it had no spiritual effect. Nor at the moment did the friends and disciples of Jesus derive anything except horror and sorrow from this to them terrible event. But later, within the Church mysteriously born out of this tragedy, the crucifixion assumed an entirely new import for those who were aware of its marvelous results in themselves and their fellow-believers. Jesus had died "for them"—a sacrifice to emancipate them from sin. We hear them taking their definition of duty from the Crucified. "Hereby know we love because he laid down his life for us." More significant still, God Himself is revealed to them in that grim cross: "God so loved the world." That brutal execution outside the walls of ancient Jerusalem became to those who experienced the transforming power of the Crucified a window through which the invisible Lord of the universe shines forth in His grace.

Henry Sloane Coffin

I. SOLDIERS AND CENTURION

201. FRAGMENT FROM GOLGOTHA

My mind is for ever splintered
on the anvil of Time
and my spirit wanders restlessly
through the caverns of Eternity.
You ask me why?

I was an ordinary legionary in Jerusalem
nigh two thousand years ago.
One chill, windy morning
we nailed a Man to a cross.
(It was a routine job.)
He died rather soon.
I remember throwing down the dice
(we were gambling for His clothes),
and, picking up my spear, a trusty weapon
that had seen me through many a skirmish
in Gaul and Libya,
I thrust it into His side
to make certain before telling the centurion.
I saw water and blood trickle down the haft
gripped in my hands.
I saw more—though, by the bird of Jupiter,
I wish I hadn't.
Looking into His deathless eyes
I saw His heart was broken
for me.

CHANDRAN DEVANESEN

202. GAMBLER

And sitting down, they watched Him there,
The soldiers did;
There, while they played with dice,
He made His sacrifice,
And died upon the cross to rid
God's world of sin.
He was a gambler, too, my Christ,
He took His life and threw
It for a world redeemed.
And ere His agony was done,
Before the westering sun went down,
Crowning that day with crimson crown,
He knew that He had won.

G. A. STUDDERT-KENNEDY

203. A RIGHTEOUS MAN

The centurion was a representative of discipline and duty. It is worthy of passing notice that every centurion mentioned in the New Testament was a good man. It was a centurion who said to Jesus: "I also am a man set under authority, having under myself soldiers: and I say to this one, Go, and he goeth; and to another, Come, and he cometh" (Luke 7:8). In that statement there is contained a remarkable philosophy of authority and discipline. I am under authority, I obey; therefore I have authority, I command others to obey. The true philosophy of human government lies within that statement. The man who has a right to rule is the man who knows how to be ruled. The only man fit to issue orders is the man accustomed to obey orders. "I am under authority, I have authority." This centurion in the presence of the Cross was a man of law, of order, of discipline, of duty, and from that standpoint of life he had watched the dying man until at last he said, "Truly this was a Son of God" (Matt. 27:54). To properly appreciate this statement we must understand the Roman thought rather than the Hebrew in the phrase "a Son of God." I believe the centurion meant that He was one of the sons of the gods. The Roman idea of God was that of heroic, courageous manhood, magnified in all its powers, and looking upon this man in His suffering, the heroism, the courage and the discipline manifested in submission, appealed to him as being Godlike.

And yet he said another thing, "Certainly this was a righteous Man" (Luke 23:47). This was the conviction of one who was himself a man of duty. To this Roman soldier the one governing principle of life was that of duty. He lived in the midst of a system. He marched in rhythm and time. He obeyed and insisted upon obedience with inflexible regularity. Rightness was the one word of value to him, at least in the sphere of his soldierhood. He saw in the Man upon the Cross One evidently acting in the realm of order, submissive to authority, and therefore authoritative, keeping time with eternal principles in the quiet majesty of His submission, "a righteous Man." The centurion as a man of duty discovered order in the Cross, and as a man who worshipped high ideals, saw the Son of God crucified.

G. CAMPBELL MORGAN

J. JOSEPH OF ARIMATHAEA

204. LIGHT AT EVENTIDE

It is significant that all the four Evangelists tell the deed of Joseph. We can understand why it was so indelibly imprinted on their memories, and was deemed so worthy of record. The day of Jesus' death had been one long sorrow and shame. From the midnight hour in Gethsemane, until Christ bowed His head in death, there had been the awful contrast between love and constancy and tender pity and holy sacrifice on the one side, and betrayal, denial, desertion, and derision on the other. But then at the close of it all, there is this brave and beautiful deed. It is a touch of tenderness after a day of unrelenting hate and cruel wrong.

"How far that little candle throws his beams,
So shines a good deed in this naughty world."

So with glad and reverent hearts these Evangelists pen the story that tells that even in so dark a day there was light at eventide.

W. M. CLOW

205. PERSONAL RESPECT

All the four writers agree that, shortly after the death of Jesus, Pilate was approached by Joseph of Arimathaea for permission to bury the body. Whatever doubts may attach, therefore, to other aspects of the tragedy it seems indisputable that this man, a person of social distinction and even of official status, so far detached himself from the Priestly party, as to seek permission to give the crucified Prisoner an honourable burial.

It is sometimes suggested that Joseph's motive in performing this act was to comply with the Jewish law with regard to burial. I find it difficult to accept this suggestion in face of the evidence. There were *three bodies to be disposed of before sunset, not one,* and there is not the slightest trace of any solicitude on the part of Joseph for the two robbers. His sole motive and preoccupation seems to have been to pay a personal and individual respect to the remains of Jesus. So far from weakening this supposition the few details given in the Gospels with regard to Joseph strengthen it. We are told that "he consented not" in the Great Sanhedrin "to the death of Christ." St. Luke says: he "was looking for the Kingdom of God." St. John, rather more explicitly, but in quite different language, says "he was a disciple, but secretly, for fear of the Jews." But great events call forth heroic traits in the character of men, and when Jesus was beyond the further pursuit of his enemies, Joseph seems to have risen to the level of his own secret aspirations. He had the courage to go to Pilate and ask for the body.

FRANK MORISON

206. CURIOUS STUDY

Joseph is a curious study. (1) It may well be that it is from Joseph that all the information about the trial before the Sanhedrin came. Certainly none of the disciples were there. The information must have come from some member of the Sanhedrin, and it is very probable that it was from Joseph that it came. If that is so Joseph had a very real share in the writing of the gospel story. (2) There is a certain tragedy about Joseph. He was a member of the Sanhedrin and yet we hear no word that he in any way spoke one word in Jesus' favour or intervened on His behalf. Joseph is the man who gave Jesus a tomb when He was dead, but who was silent when He was alive. It is one of the commonest tragedies of life that we keep our wreaths for people's graves and orations and praises until they are dead. It would be infinitely better to give them some of these flowers and some of these words of gratitude when they are still alive. (3) But we cannot blame Joseph overmuch, for Joseph was another of these people for whom the Cross of Jesus did what not even the life of Jesus could do. When he had seen Jesus alive he had felt His attraction, but had gone no further. But when he saw Jesus die—and he must have been present at the crucifixion— his heart was broken in love. First the centurion, then Joseph—it is an amazing thing how soon Jesus' words came true that when He was lifted up from the earth He would draw all men unto Him (John 12: 32).

WILLIAM BARCLAY

207. JOSEPH OF ARIMATHAEA

Did Joseph have a feeling of regret:
Perhaps some word unsaid—some deed undone,
That made him come in tenderness to get
Christ's body from the cross? Yet he was one
Who was a counsellor, called good and just,
And still the good and just can sometimes fail . . .
He must have winced when thinking of the thrust
Of thorny crown—flesh pierced by cruel nail.

I think he knelt with chastened, contrite heart,
To wrap the body in its linen shroud,
And hoped this act would somehow heal the smart
Of past neglect, and being thus allowed
The task, perhaps it helped him to atone—
That he found peace beside that tomb of stone.

MARGARET E. BRUNER

208. IN BEHALF OF JOSEPH

Joseph has figured in many sermons as a "twilight disciple" or a "disciple in the dark." He has been called that on the ground that he did nothing until after Jesus was dead, and then not until darkness had fallen. This has been manifestly unfair to Joseph. The failures of secret discipleship, of discipleship in the dark, which acts "too little and too late," and never dares the open discipleship of the sunlight, are great. Warnings against it are always in order. But such sermons ought not to be attached to Joseph of Aritmathaea. . . . It took real courage to do what he did, to disregard the angry Jews and face Pilate with a request for the body of Jesus. Joseph is to be held in honor, not in reproach.

HALFORD E. LUCCOCK

VI. Day of Crucifixion

A. HE STANDS ON TRIAL

209. AN IRREGULAR TRIAL

When we consider the character of the men who demanded the death of Jesus Christ and the conditions upon which they made their demand, we conclude at once that prejudice controlled those responsible every step of the way as they went about to secure his death. When we know their laws and customs, we are astonished that a people who were as law-loving and law-abiding would allow their laws to be broken and their legal precedents to be thrown aside as was done when they were seeking means to secure the death of Jesus Christ.

Jesus was tried a number of times but all his trials were irregular, partisan, illegal. He could be tried in one of three places: where he was born, where he had his residence, or where his crime was supposed to have been committed. He was born in Bethlehem but he was tried in Jerusalem. His natural residence was Nazareth and his Jewish residence recognized by the Roman government was Bethlehem, but he was tried in Jerusalem. His accusers charged him with sedition committed in Galilee but he was tried in Judea. No formal charge was made against him and therefore they had no right to arrest him. No advocate was appointed to appear for him and therefore he had no fair trial. His judges were prejudiced against him. They hired witnesses to testify against him. They announced their decision before they heard the case. They convened their court at night when their law forbade it so to convene for the purpose of a trial for a capital offense. They also, contrary to their law, sat in session on a feast day. It was the unusual procedure for the youngest member to speak first and then in regular order according to age, and then the High Priest would speak, gathering up the argument and pronouncing sentence. In the trial of Jesus the High Priest was one of the first to speak and, after hearing the answer of Jesus to a certain question, the High Priest broke their law by rending his garment. It was required that twenty-four hours intervene between a sentence and its execution. That period was a time of grace when new evidence was to be sought and time spent in fasting and prayer. The record of Jesus' ecclesiastical trial does not indicate that any such period of time intervened. Certainly there was no fasting nor prayer. So far as the ecclesiastical trials of Jesus were concerned, they were a mere travesty on authority and had little semblance of order.

C. H. STAUFFACHER

210. DAY OF DECISION

It was not Jesus who was on trial before Pilate; it was the Jewish religion, it was the Roman Empire, it was human justice, on trial before Jesus. Pilate was judged for ever there and then by Jesus; and so were the priests, and the people who shouted for Barabbas, some because they wanted him, and some because they did not like to say anything else; and so were all the men and women whose lives were shaped and determined, as they looked at Jesus on the Cross that day. That principle always holds. A man writes himself down when he says he does not like a great work of art, drama, or music, or picture. We exhibit our own characters in our judgments of Jesus Christ; we label ourselves, and, what is more, we give a turn to our development for good or ill. Pilate and Caiaphas and the rest had been, like all men, developing character in the ordinary way—by choices, inclinations, and fancies, by tacit acceptances of principles of life. This day suddenly and forever declared what type of men they had chosen to be, or had become by that negligence, which after all is a choice too. And, as already suggested, the day confirmed their choices and fixed their characters; they accepted themselves more definitely as they stood. The attitude of every man that day was partly the outcome of his former life and so revealed it; but it was also a new self-determination brought about by the contact of the character he had developed with something wholly new, a new situation, a new type, and so it became decisive for the future. The day was as decisive for the other onlookers, for those who wept, for those who looked away and would not see, for Simon the Cyrenian whom (and his sons after him) it brought into the circle of Jesus' followers. And the day was decisive for mankind; if it was to be a choice between Pilate and Jesus, then God's universe must fit and match one of them, and that one could hardly be Pilate. Pilate's universe will not do.

T. R. GLOVER

211. THE CHARGE AGAINST HIM

The Romans placed . . . a "titulus" around the neck of a condemned criminal, or on his cross, to state the charge against him. Though the Gospels disagree as to whether this inscription contained Jesus' name, they all agree that the accusation read, "King of the Jews," and John tells us that it was written "in Hebrew, in Latin, and in Greek" (19: 20; cf. some manuscripts of Lk. 23:38). Thus Pilate not only declared Jesus a rebel pretender, but also both insulted and threatened the Jews. The placard seemed to say to them, "See the kind of King you have!"—and also, "Thus will the Romans deal with any Jew who tries to seize independent power!" The chief priests' resentment of the insult is made explicit in the Fourth Gospel by their fruitless effort to have Pilate alter the inscription to read, "This man said, I am King of the Jews" (Jn. 19:21 f.).

WALLACE EUGENE ROLLINS
MARION BENEDICT ROLLINS

212. THE INESCAPABLE JESUS

The trial before Pilate dramatizes the inescapable Jesus. Pilate did not ask for this trial. It was thrust upon him. He found Jesus on his hands, and he did not know what to do about it. Pilate tried every way possible to evade the issue. He first suggested to the Jews that they try Jesus, since Jesus was a Jew. But they said that they were not empowered to put him to death. Then Pilate sent Jesus to Herod for trial. But Herod promptly sent him back to Pilate. Then Pilate tried to substitute Barabbas for Jesus. But the people would have none of it. Pilate then asked them if they wanted him to crucify their own king, the king of the Jews. But the priests had an answer for that one. "We have no king but Caesar." Finally in desperation Pilate puts the fatal question to the crowd. "What shall I then do with Jesus?" When the crowd cried out for crucifixion, Pilate released Jesus to them. But as a last effort to get the matter off his conscience, Pilate washed his hands, hoping thus to rid himself of any blame for Jesus' death.

CHARLES M. CROWE

213. OPEN VISION

Have you not gazed in wonder at the sight of Christ before His judges? How calm and self-possessed He was, far more self-possessed than Caiaphas, or Pilate, or Herod, or any of the other actors on that tragic stage. What was the secret of it? Was it just His innate heroism asserting itself? Was it just Christ's way of steeling His heart to be brave? Was it only a reckless contempt of death? No. It was the open vision that behind Caiaphas, and behind Pilate, and behind Herod, there was Someone else; and that it was not they nor any earthly governor who reigned in Jerusalem that night, but that Other, that watching, brooding Figure among the shadows—God! And Caiaphas, Pilate, Herod—who or what were they? Less than the dust beneath time's chariot-wheels.

JAMES S. STEWART

B. GOOD FRIDAY

214. TOO GREAT FOR WORDS

On Good Friday, 1500 years ago, Bishop Ambrose ascended his pulpit in the Cathedral of Milan and addressed his congregation in the following words: "I find it impossible to speak to you today. The events of Good Friday are too great for human words. Why should I speak while my Saviour is silent and dies?" Every preacher of the Cross has had this experience, especially when he compares the weakness of his own words with the majesty and power of the seven short sentences which our Lord spoke in the six hours from nine o'clock in the morning until three o'clock in the afternoon. With these seven words we enter the Holy of Holies of the plans of God for men.

O. P. KRETZMANN

215. BOWING IN ADORATION

In some moods—the mood, for example, in which I find myself on each Good Friday morning—one feels it almost a sacrilege to argue and to discuss. One desires then only to bow in adoration before the mystery of a love whose depths no one can sound and the range of whose august purposes is like that of a shooting star. It sweeps in from the Infinite and the Unknown, and comes near enough to earth so that we may see something of its shining glory. We watch with awe and wonder; but when all that can be seen by human eyes has passed into the darkness, and a cry is heard, "It is finished," we still know that a purpose goes on, beyond our vision, in the Infinite and the Unknown, and we cannot even imagine its scope or guess at its goal.

LESLIE D. WEATHERHEAD

216. APPROPRIATE THOUGHTS

This is a very solemn day; for on this day the Lord Jesus Christ was crucified. The question for us is, how ought we to keep it? That is, what sort of thoughts ought to be in our minds upon this day? Now, many most excellent and pious persons, and most pious books, seem to think that we ought to-day to think as much as possible of the sufferings of our blessed Lord; and because we cannot, of course, understand or imagine the sufferings of His Spirit, to think of what we can, that is, His bodily sufferings. They, therefore, seem to wish to fill our minds with the most painful pictures of agony, and shame, and death, and sorrow. . . . Now, I judge no man; to his own master he standeth or falleth; yea, and he shall stand, for God is able to make him stand. But it does seem to me that these good people are seeking the living among the dead, and forgetting that Christ is neither on the cross nor in the tomb, but that He is risen.

CHARLES KINGSLEY

217. WHAT THE DAY MEANS

This is what Good Friday means: God in Christ reconciling the world unto Himself, not from outside as if just stooping down from above

93

but from within the process of human life, charging it with strange, new possibilities of achievement. And the identification of the Son of God with this life of ours comes to its completion as death itself is made the means by which He penetrates to the very heart of human existence.

HUGHELL E. W. FOSBROKE

218. GOOD FRIDAY

We who have loved—today we bring
Love's flask, filled full of ointment sweet,
And break it at Thy nail-torn feet—
Counting the cost, in terms of Spring,
A very tiny, trifling thing.

We who have fought—today we lay
The fallen flag, the shattered sword,
Upon Thine altar steps, O Lord,
Beside the victor's wreath of bay,
Commemorating Calvary.

We who have failed—today we hear
The broken echo of a cry
From a far Cross—"Eli, Eli! . . ."
Before the skies are rent with fear
And Death becomes Life's victory!

JOHNSTONE G. PATRICK

219. THREE HOURS DEVOTION

The purpose of the Three Hours Devotion is not to revel in feeling, or to indulge in a kind of spiritual sadism, concentrating steadily (or even repeatedly) upon our Lord's sufferings. "Do not weep for me," he told the women of Jerusalem, as they saw him led to execution, "but weep for yourselves and for your children" (Luke 23:28). He does not ask our sympathy, as a great actor appeals to the deep feelings of his audience. For after all this is no spectacle, no drama of some mythical or legendary hero (like Oedipus or Prometheus or Mithras), but the story of a man who lived and died in Judea—"under Pontius Pilate," as the Creed says. It is meant, not to stir our surface feelings, but to reach the very depths of our souls—and transform them. The old rule for meditation is a good one to follow: Picture the scene, Study the teaching, Draw the inference, Charge the will. Imagination alone is not enough—that is only the beginning. The activity of thought, the use of the mind, the function of logic, the practical conclusion, the decision, the act of the will—all this is equally involved, if we are really to profit by the purifying, purging experience of deep and genuine devotion.

FREDERICK C. GRANT

C. WORDS FROM THE CROSS

220. ENGRAVED ON THE HEART

The words of the world's great men and women have been recorded after them. Many of these words, phrases, and expressions are found engraved upon marble slabs and monuments. Others are found painted in the most imperishable, yet delicate, colors of art; while others are chronicled in the numberless books of the libraries of civilization. Man has attempted to preserve every word which has fallen from the lips of the Son of God. Upon the hearts of Christian men are engraved, chiseled, and chronicled in deepest devotion and highest reverence the words of Christ from Calvary, called "The Seven Words of Christ from His Cross." These words are so chaste, so reasonable, so human, so divine, so holy, and so supreme. To live in their company for forty days, for forty years, for a lifetime is sufficient to bring about a personal transformation within the lives of men.

EDWARD JEFFRIES REES

221. WORDS FROM HIS LIPS

We see in the Cross what we have the eyes to see. The scribes and Pharisees saw in it the end of a heretic. The Romans saw in it the end of one who trifles with the law. The soldiers saw a fanatic who had stirred up his fanatical people. The disciples saw in it the loss of their

Friend and Master; some thought it premature and unnecessary; few if any understood what was happening. Perhaps His mother alone knew that this was more stupendous than any of them realized. It needed the thought of St. Paul, and the long perspective of history, for men to begin to understand something of what had happened. It is for us today just another good Man sacrificing Himself for His cause; or it is the most significant event on all the plane of human history, an event with cosmic significance for the relations between the holy and living God, and sinful, guilty humanity; and therefore with personal and eternal significance for you and me. On the Cross we watch that all taking place. We hear some of the words that fall from His lips in this hour of His humiliation and of His supreme glory. He is sharing with us, and letting us share with Him.

SAMUEL M. SHOEMAKER

222. GODWARD AND MANWARD ASPECTS

Our Lord was both God and man, and His words and deeds have, therefore, both a Godward and a manward aspect. From the manward point of view, His utterances on Calvary tell us of the human side of His Passion: of His suffering, of His patient endurance, of His thoughtfulness, of His mental and spiritual struggle, of His self-surrender. From the Godward point of view, they tell us of the blessings which God has in store for us. The two points of view are closely related, so closely that we can scarcely think of one apart from the other. Yet inevitably we place the emphasis on one or the other. . . . I should like to place it on the Godward point of view. . . . The first word suggests Our Hope of Pardon; the second, Our Hope of Heaven; the third, Our Hope of Understanding; the fourth, Our Hope of Victory; the fifth, Our Hope of Resurrection; the sixth, Our Hope of Achievement; the seventh, Our Hope of Peace.

J. WILSON SUTTON

1. "Father, Forgive . . ."

223. WHO IS FORGIVEN?

This . . . prayer of our Lord, "Father, forgive them . . ." constitutes one of the "seven words" from the cross. It is traditionally supposed to have been uttered while the soldiers were driving the nails through his hands and feet. Therefore it has been suggested that the words should be taken as applying only to these men who were merely doing their duty. That is to narrow their application unjustifiably. Is it not in keeping with all that we know of the mind and spirit of Jesus to believe that they were intended to apply to all who had any part or lot in the events that brought about his death on the cross, whether or not they had any hand in the actual crucifixion? May we not truly believe that Jesus had in mind Pilate, the undecided and vacillating Roman; Herod, the crafty Jew; Annas and Caiaphas, the priests, blind leaders of the blind; the scribes and the Pharisees, with their false worship of tradition; and all the rest of the unnamed ones who for one reason or another felt that Jesus meant danger to them, and that it was expedient he should die and so trouble them no more?

JOHN TREVOR DAVIES

224. ATTITUDE TOWARD SINNERS

"They know not what they do." The example of Jesus gives us the pattern of our attitude towards those who sin, particularly towards those who sin against us. There is here no outbreak of righteous indignation, no easy denunciation. Jesus shows only pity for those who are evil. That He could be angry with self-satisfied sinners we know; but anger and condemnation are not incompatible with pity. We should not allow that "indignation against successful vice," of which Bishop Butler speaks, to drive out compassion for the wrongdoer. The attitude of Jesus is indeed heroic, but nonetheless sane and reasonable. Surely no reflective man can have acted as a judge of others without wondering how far the culprits whom he condemned were fully aware of what they did. What strange obscurations of the mind overtook them, what pall of ignorance surrounded them perhaps from their childhood? We cannot enter into the minds of others or weigh their motives or their opportunities. While he administers the rough justice of men which the protection of society requires, the judge must sometimes rejoice to think that there is a higher justice which can look upon the heart, and a Judge who tries men by the standard of Jesus.

W. R. MATTHEWS

225. HIS PRIESTLY OFFICE

This prayer should teach us, first of all, that our dear Lord Jesus is a priest, and that He fulfilled the duties of His priestly office there upon the cross. To pray for sinners is, indeed, one of the proper employments of the priesthood. Now, Aaron, serving under the law, was invested with peculiar priestly apparel made for glory and for beauty. But would we know with what priestly robes Christ was clad and what the altar was at which He served, we need merely look at the cross. There we see Him entirely naked, full of wounds and void of every trace of sacerdotal splendor. Still He attended to His priestly duties most perfectly and carefully, even praying for His foes. Let us not be offended at His unpriestly appearance, for the work of this Priest has a significance entirely different from that of Moses' priests. This difference we learn even from the superscription written over Him, which declares Him to be "The King of the Jews," the correctness of which title He had himself publicly and clearly confessed before Pilate.

Martin Luther

2. "Today in Paradise"

226. LIGHT FROM HEAVEN

In these verses (Luke 23:39-43) we have an example of the interesting way in which the evangelists, without contradicting, supplement each other. In the fourth gospel, in a manner not like its usual style where it touches on points already reported, we find, instead of any addition, the briefest statement of the fact anywhere given; for it simply tells us, that our Lord had two others crucified with Him: "On either side one and Jesus in the midst," without saying a word as to their character. The first and second evangelists add to our knowledge, for they state that these persons were malefactors (thieves or robbers), and that they took part with the multitude in reviling the Saviour. This might have been all that we ever learned: and in that case the information, though scanty, would have been far from uninstructive. It would have confirmed by another feature the accuracy of the crucifixion narrative, as we know from other sources, that crucifixion was a punishment to which numbers were condemned together. It would have fulfilled a part of the most remarkable of all Old Testament prophecies respecting the Messiah: "And He was numbered with the transgressors." It would have illustrated the malignity of our Lord's enemies in appointing Him such persons as His companions in dying, and in placing Him between them as the worst criminal of the three. Nor would it have failed to bring out the depravity of the race for which the Saviour died, as capable of insulting even an innocent fellow-sufferer in death, whether in wantonness or in the hope of aggravating personal agony.

All these lessons would have remained, had the Gospel of Luke never been written at all. There is nothing discordant: but how new is the impression which these few touches give! What in the other gospels is like a beacon set up to warn is converted into a trophy of redeeming grace, and a beam of light so sweet and cheering, as to have come only direct from heaven, is let in upon the mortal darkness of the crucifixion.

JOHN CAIRNS

227. WHY AND HOW THEY SUFFERED

Three crosses stood on Calvary's brow. One man died there because he loved. Two died because they hated. One hated to the end. Another renounced hatred and surrendered to love. The scene is a final picture of the eternal opposition of love and hatred. Love includes all the virtues; hatred includes all the vices. The conflict between Good and Evil ultimately narrows to a titanic struggle between these two forces.

Physical suffering was equally real for the three men on Calvary's three crosses. The difference lay in why they suffered and how they suffered. Jesus was crucified because he loved men, because he sought to give life, because he dared resist evil. The two thieves were crucified because they hated men, because they sought to take life, and because they dared resist good. Hatred incarnated in them attempted to destroy love incarnated in Jesus. Thus, though the thieves shared the suffering with him, they also caused his suffering. Evil kills both its friends and its foes. It is death; it can never give life. Good is life; it can never take life. Hatred and love are the processes of life-taking and life-giving.

TALMAGE C. JOHNSON

228. HE REPRESENTS MANKIND

As far as the Gospel record is concerned, seemingly out of nowhere the character of the penitent thief is plummeted into the crucifixion scene: nameless, too, except for tradition, which calls him Dismas. The lack of definite information of this character, to whom this second Word from the Cross is addressed, has been the cue for some unwarranted speculation, as well as the use of a too unbridled imagination in attempting to reconstruct a story of his life from which to deduce some lessons of instruction and warning to Christians of all generations.

He has been variously called by the Gospel writers: a thief, a robber, a malefactor. Other students have inferred, and not without warrant, that he was a political revolutionary, and belonged to one of the many guerilla bands of political enthusiasts, who were keeping alive the hope of breaking the strange hold of Rome. He was now expiating his crime as an insurrectionist. He may have been any one of these, or all of them together, and a great deal more. All these designations of the kind of a man he may have been suggest a life of violence. The important thing to remember is, he was not a good man, a moral man. In fact, by his own admission, he together with his companion, on the other side of Jesus, are now reaping the just reward of their misdeeds. In short, he was as bad as any man could possibly be, according to the judgment of society's law, which was now exacting from him the price of his high criminality.

By the ligitimate use of imagination, whose legitimacy may be attested by the spirit of the Gospel, we may infer that the Gospel writer, with deliberate intent, left this "thief" nameless, simply because he *represents* in this scene *every member of the human race*. He might have your name or mine.

LOUIS A. SITTLER

229. UPON A HILL

Three men shared death upon a hill,
But only one man dies;
The other two—
A thief and God Himself—
Made rendezvous.

Three crosses still
Are borne up Calvary's Hill,
Where Sin still lifts them high:
Upon the one, sag broken men
Who, cursing, die;
Another holds the praying thief,
Or those who penitent as he,
Still find the Christ
Beside them on the tree.

Miriam LeFevre Crouse

3. "Woman . . . Son"

230. NATURAL RELATIONSHIPS

It is a homely, a private, and individual word which occupies our attention. It is none the less instructive and inspiring on that account for us who are nothing if we are not homely, who are members of families, with our close relationships, mothers and sons, fathers and daughters, sisters and brothers, husbands and wives. It is deeply touching to us to find that our Lord in His agony has something to say on these natural relationships; nay, rather, that He takes special care even then to set us an example of what sons should be to their mothers and the like. It is the glory of our religion that it has something to say to us on all our natural duties. It is the glory of our religion that it takes all our natural duties and transforms them so far as they are base and selfish, and ennobles them so far as they are pure and true. Theological duties, if we may so call them, and natural duties are intertwined the one with the other for us Christians. If a man love God, he must love his brother also. If a man love not his brother, he cannot love his God. We get our inspiration whether of love to God or of love to our fellowman from one and the same source—the love passing knowledge of Him who is at once God and Man; and where does that love shine more brightly than at the Cross? He who lived as a man amongst men teaches us how to live as men amongst men, as members of families united by bonds of natural love. And never does He teach us more persuasively than when, in this Third Word from the Cross, He speaks to us not so much as a priest, or a king, but as a man.

FREDERIC WATSON

231. HE SANCTIFIED THE HOME

On many counts Jesus is compared with the Athenian martyr, Socrates. In connection with the Third Word there comes to mind the story Plato tells of Socrates' death. The condemned Athenian's wife, Xanthippe, came to see him. Always a peevish, uncontrolled creature, Xanthippe was sobbing violently. "Take her away!" was the response of her blasé husband; "if she stays here crying so hysterically, I may not be able to die with the calmness which befits a philosopher."

"Take her away!" The Son of God has many superiorities over the Greek Socrates, not least of which is Jesus' response to the woman nearest Him in human relationship, when she stood by the Cross mourning His untimely sacrifice. "Behold thy son!" He said to her— and thus sanctified the home not only in His birth, His childhood obedience, and His manhood support, but also in His death.

THEODORE K. FINCK

232. A MOTHER'S SACRIFICE

The sacrifice of the cross is the sacrifice of Jesus. But it was the sacrifice of the Father likewise "who spared not His own Son, but delivered Him up for us all." And it was also the sacrifice of Mary, who stood in meek acquiescence to see her Son die. This sacrifice of Mary has been finely conceived by Holman Hunt. He has drawn the carpenter's shop at Nazareth. Jesus stands at His bench with uplifted arms, as though in a moment of aspiration, and Mary stooping behind Him, sees the shadow of His arms cast on a wall before Him. To her foreboding heart, it is the shadow of a cross. It is a fine suggestion of the chilling fear which early possessed her heart, and because a heavier sorrow as

He passed onward in His ministry, and now was realized in this dying hour. "A sword shall pierce their own heart also," Simon had prophesied. Now standing by the cross she felt its sharp thrust, and she bowed her head as she made the mother's last sacrifice. "The Lord gave, and the Lord hath taken away; blessed be the name of the Lord," was the psalm that she chanted in spirit.

W. M. CLOW

4. "My God, Why?"

233. MEETING THE DARKNESS

To many of us this Word is more precious than any of the others, and has more comfort in it even than those which speak of triumph and final peace. For we find here that Jesus can be our companion and leader just when we need Him most. He has passed through the "dark night of the soul," and He has known what it means to look round on the world, and into the mind itself, and find no sign of God's working or any answer to our heart's petition.

He shows us the way in which we can meet the darkness, we in our little passions as He in His great one. We may direct our attention to the stores of our memory. We are too much the victims of our moods. Now the sky is dark and God's presence not discernible; but are we just creatures of this passing moment? This moment is not the whole of our lives, and what we think and feel now does not represent the whole of ourselves. We have had moments when we knew that God was the foundation of our life, and when it was clear to us that our aspirations after good were not attempts to clasp illusions. When the hour of darkness descends upon us, we will remember the days that are past. The storehouse of memory is worth keeping well filled, experience of spiritual reality when it comes to us is worth dwelling upon and keeping fresh in our recollection, because there may be a day when, for a time, we shall have to nourish our souls on what they have laid in store.

Most people miss the support which they might have had in the day of doubt because they insist on being solitary. When God grew dim to Jesus He remembered that God was throned upon the praises of Israel. While we look out at the world and life through our own little window and refuse to listen to the reports of others about what they have seen from theirs, we lack the support which we might have. It is only a tiny fragment, after all, that each one of us can see from his window. But we are not alone. Like Jesus, we may be supported by the choir invisible of those who have known the reality of God in their own experience.

W. R. MATTHEWS

234. HE DECLARES FOR GOD

He could not see, could not feel Him near; and yet it is *"My* God" that He cries. Thus the will of Jesus, in the very moment when His faith seems about to yield, is finally triumphant. It has no *feeling* now to support it, no beatific vision to absorb it. It stands naked in His soul and tortured, as He stood naked and scourged before Pilate. Pure and simple and surrounded by fire, it declares for God.

GEORGE MACDONALD

235. OUR SAVIOUR'S AGONY

To be the Light of the world and to be not only rejected but reviled, spit on, crucified, to offer salvation to men who are perishing and in return to be crowned with thorns and hung between two thieves; to be the well-beloved of God and to give oneself utterly to his purposes, and then to find those purposes seeming to miscarry; to hang in the darkness between heaven and earth and in a blinding agony of pain to seem to belong to neither; to feel the impact of sin and to look into the bottomless pit, to be sinking to death and to feel no support of the Everlasting Arms—all these we glimpse of the Saviour's agony; all these we sense in the hollow and awful tones, "My God, my God, why hast thou forsaken me?"

LESLIE BADHAM

236. SIN, SORROW, AND SILENCE

These words reveal a mystery, and represent in mystery a revelation. To them we turn for a theory of the Atonement, only to discover that theorizing is impossible. Alone in the supreme hour in the history of the race, Christ uttered these words, and in them light breaks out, and yet merges, not into darkness, but into light so blinding that no eye can bear to gaze. The words are recorded, not to finally reveal, but to reveal so much as it is possible for men to know, and to set a limit at the point where men may never know. The words were uttered that men may know, and that men may know how much there is that may not be known. In that strange cry that broke from the lips of the Master there are at least three things perfectly clear. Let them be named and considered. It is the cry of One who has reached the final issue of sin. It is the cry of One who has fathomed the deepest depth of sorrow. It is the cry of One Himself o'erwhelmed in the mystery of silence. Sin, sorrow, silence. Sin at its final issue, sorrow at its deepest depth, silence the unexplainable mystery of agony, and agony of mystery. These are the facts suggested by the actual words.

G. CAMPBELL MORGAN

237. WITH TRUST AND PRAISE

The one word from the Cross in Mark-Matthew is the most difficult of all to interpret: "My God, my God, why hast thou forsaken me?" (Mk. 15:34; Mt. 27:46). Was this a temporary resurgence of the Gethsemane struggle? Or had Jesus, in his vicarious self-offering as the Suffering Servant, so identified himself with those for whom he suffered that the weight of their sin broke for a moment that sensitive spirit? To many scholars, this "cry of dereliction" has seemed the most certainly authentic of the recorded words from the Cross. Yet the whole meaning of Psalm 22 has led other interpreters to believe that this was not a cry of despair. The psalmist, who began his prayer thus went on to describe his desertion and reproaches by all men, finally moved out of his pleading into trust and praise. Since devout Jews used this psalm in times of adversity, many commentators believe that "no pious Israelite, dying with these words upon his lips, could be thought—or could have thought himself—to be abandoned by God." It also seems to many very improbable that either Mark or Matthew would have reported a word that the Evangelist himself regarded as a dying cry of desolation.

WALLACE EUGENE ROLLINS
MARION BENEDICT ROLLINS

5. *"I Thirst"*

238. MORE THAN PHYSICAL THIRST

Can it be *Jesus* who uttered these words? Yes; for his death was real, as his life was real. The author of the Gospel of John insists upon the utter reality of Jesus' life and death, from the beginning to the end of his book. Christ was no God in disguise, traveling the earth incognito, a phantom or a transient epiphany of the deity (as in the tales of the pagan gods)—one who could not suffer because he was divine. The Gospel of John is deeply and steadily concerned to assert and to vindicate the truth that Jesus' human life was real, even his physical life. For there was a strange sect at that time, the "Docetists," who denied that Christ "had come in the flesh."

And yet the words must mean much more than physical thirst. Jesus thirsted for life: he was young, scarcely thirty. And thirsted for the souls of men: "My son, give me thine heart." And he longed to quench the thirst in the souls of other men: "I came that they may have life, and have it abundantly" (John 10:10). To the woman at the well near Samaria he had offered this boon: "Every one who drinks of this water will thirst again, but whoever drinks of the water that I shall give him will never thirst" (John 4:13-14). "If any one thirst, let him come to me, and let him who believes in me drink. As the scripture has said, 'Out of his heart shall flow rivers of living water'" (John 7:37-38, RSV mg.)

> 'Tis life, whereof our nerves are scant, . . .
> More life, and fuller, that I want.

And if he too thirsted for life, he had the assurance of life beyond life.

FREDERICK C. GRANT

239. HIS PRAYER TO MEN

Jesus did not utter this word, as a superficial reading of the text might suggest, in order to fulfill the scriptures. Had such been the case, our Lord would have been little better than an actor, and he never put on an act. The assertion "that the scripture might be fulfilled" is the affirmation of a result rather than of a purpose. If Jesus did not utter this word to fulfill the scriptures, still less did he utter it as an appeal for pity. Jesus hated being pitied, as strong souls ever do. It was because of this hatred that he rebuked those women who sobbed over him as he journeyed to his cross. No more was this a grim bulletin announcing how the sufferer was faring as he did his last mile. Least of all was it a half-crazed cry that agony surprised from his unwilling lips.

Jesus was fully conscious of saying this word, as he was of saying every other word that he spoke upon his cross. Indeed we may be certain that the principal reason for his refusing the medicated wine that was offered him before his crucifixion was that he might meet his ordeal intellectually alert and alive. He was determined to keep his faculties unbeclouded to the very end. This he did. Therefore Jesus knew exactly what he was saying when he cried, "I thirst."

In my opinion he was here once more engaged in prayer. But this prayer he offered, not to his Father, but to men. What is stranger still, he offered it to men who, either in cruel indifference or in vindictive hate, were making his last moments as bitter as possible. If this is a prayer, what an amazing prayer this is! It is also as beautiful as it is amazing.

CLOVIS G. CHAPPELL

240. CHRIST CALLS FOR HELP

The strong Son of God hung dying on the cross. His lips and His throat were parched. He called for help, "I thirst." Whom did He call? Did an angel descend to aid Him? It was a soldier of the Roman legion who answered our Savior's cry of need. Only when a person is unable to help himself can he, with self-respect, ask another's aid. Even the eternal Christ, who had laid aside His power and glory and hung helpless on the cross, did not think it below His dignity to call upon a man for help.

No man can finally rely upon himself. Each of us is a unit in the body of mankind. Each of us depends upon others. God brought us into the world through the agency of human parents, and a host of ancestors. Each of us grew in an environment, surrounded by all sorts of people who made a direct contribution to his life. We live in human society. The Christian contributes to society, and likewise he receives. Sometimes we Christians are most reluctant to admit how much we depend upon our fellow man.

ANDREW W. BLACKWOOD, JR.

6. *"It Is Finished"*

241. ALL HE COULD DO

The purpose of God in the history of man was accomplished when Jesus breathed His last upon the cross. The cry "It is finished" was not the mere gasp of a wornout life; it was not the cry of satisfaction with which a career of pain and sorrow is terminated; it was the deliberate utterance of a clear consciousness on the part of God's appointed Revealer that now all had been done that could be done to make God known to men and to identify Him with men. God's purpose had ever been one and indivisible—declared to men in various ways, a hint here, a broad light there, now by a gleam of insight in the mind of a prophet, now by a deed of heroism in king or leader, through rude symbolic contrivances and through the tenderest of human affections and the highest human thoughts. God had been making men ever more and more sensible that His one purpose was to come closer and closer into fellowship with them, and to draw them into a perfect harmony with Him. Forgiveness and deliverance from sin were provided for them, knowledge of God's law and will, that they might learn to know and to serve Him—all these were secured when Jesus cried, "It is finished."

MARCUS DODS

242. COMPLETE FULFILLMENT

This cry of Jesus is not just one of relief, as if he were thankful that life's sorrowful journey was at an end. The Greek word "finished" means not simply "over and done with," but "brought to a complete fulfillment." It corresponds to a saying found in our Lord's great high priestly prayer, "I have finished the work which thou gavest me to do."

How strange this almost joyous word of fulfillment must have sounded in the ears of those who were standing by, especially of those who, like the priests and Pharisees, had followed the ministry of Jesus with hostile intent. For here was a young man who had not reached what we think of today as the prime of life, coming, apparently, to an untimely end in the company of criminals, and yet, with his dying breath, declaring that he was content because he had fulfilled his life's destiny.

HUGHELL E. W. FOSBROKE

243. HIS WORK COMPLETED

We surely cannot overestimate the great importance and clearness of the fact that Jesus looked Himself for the most mighty results to issue from His dying. The great importance which the Christian Church has given to that event has only echoed the infinite estimate He set upon it. He was always pointing forward to it before it came. He met it with the most awful reverence when it arrived. And with the last gasp of His closing agony He announced the completion as if it were the work of the world that had been finished.

PHILLIPS BROOKS

244. WHAT WAS FINISHED?

What was finished? The greatest of the world's teachings from the Master Mind of time. What was finished? The last word had been stated of the great principles, that if followed out would usher in earth's golden age. What was finished? The completion of the revelation of God to man—the last word in religion had been uttered. But what was finished? The perfect life of the perfect Son of Man. From that time on, all ages have before them the example and the inspiration of an ideal—an ideal that was faultless and that challenges their admiration and spurs them to their best in the attempt to follow him. What is finished? The possibility of man's full salvation had been made. What was finished? The infinite God had gone to the limit of his own infinite power in his efforts for the benefit of men by making the fullest incarnation of himself possible in human form.

JOHN D. RHOADES

245. ACCOMPLISHED!

When Jesus uttered the words, "It is finished!" He did so as a ship's commander might utter them to his first officer as a perilous voyage through dark and menacing seas ended in a friendly harbor. One glad exultant word in His native tongue sprang to His lips: "Finished!" "Accomplished!" His life perfected, His mission was fulfilled. History confirms the verdict. "He will never be surpassed," said Renan. "Higher has human thought not reached," mused Carlyle. Before the perfection of His personality it is absurd to speak of still fuller perfection. When a perfect chord in music is played, do we expect to hear a more perfect chord? Is not Christ, to use Robert Browning's phrase, "the C Major of this life"? On the Cross, His character, His life, His disclosure of God were perfected, brought to a successful issue. Our fathers dwelt lovingly on this thought. They spoke frequently of the "finished work of the Redeemer."

DAVID A. MACLENNAN

246. THE QUESTION

I saw the Son of God go by
  Crowned with the crown of thorn.
"Was It not finished, Lord?" I said,
  "And all the anguish borne?"

He turned on me His awful eyes:
  "Hast thou not understood?
Lo! Every soul is Calvary,
  And every sin a Rood."

RACHEL ANNAND TAYLOR

7. *"Into Thy Hands"*

247. HE PERCEIVED GOD

The pain of the cross, the darkness on the cross, the evil that led to the cross, all these raise problems that are tremendous. They have always raised problems. "We preach Christ crucified," writes St. Paul,

110

"unto the Jews a stumblingblock, and unto the Greeks foolishness." They could see neither reason nor right in this case of failure and death.

But if we really want to know the nature and the character of the Power which produced and sustains life, we must account for the beauty and the wonder, the power and the glory of a Spirit that has transformed a cross of death into a symbol of life, we must account for the goodness of a Love whose outstretched arms upon a cross draws and stirs and upholds men today as it has through the centuries. If we really want to understand what manner of world this world of ours is, we must needs think of it as a world whose meaning embraces the life that blazed out into the light on the face of Jesus Christ.

He saw all the evil that we see and more. He saw pain. He looked square into the face of failure and death. And he saw beyond them to the heart of things. He perceived God. He said, "Father, into thy hands I commend my spirit."

PHILEMON F. STURGES

248. SELF-SURRENDER TO GOD

The last word of Jesus from the Cross is the last word of Christianity's wisdom for the world: self-surrender to God. "Father, into thy hands I commend my spirit." It is not resignation, nor world-weariness, nor despair: it is a profound knowledge that the heart of life, and its secret, is not in a view of the world, but in a right relationship with God. That relationship brings strength for the battles of life, and peace for the pain, and light for the questions. Faith is not conception nor attitude, faith is relationship. That is why we learn so much more about religion from human relationships, and from prayer, than we ever do merely by thinking or studying.

SAMUEL M. SHOEMAKER

249. THE LIGHT OF GOD'S PRESENCE

When the end came, Jesus turned away from the temptation to be concerned with his physical being. He set his face toward the light of

111

God's presence. "Father, into thy hands I commend my spirit," he whispered. Already he had glimpsed the glory of life as it was to be shared with his heavenly Father.

This message is dramatically pictured in an altar painting by Matthias Grunewald in the chapel in Isenheim, Germany. The altar has double wings which fold over and conceal it. The method of construction offers the artist the opportunity to paint not only the central panel and the interior surface of the open wings, but the exterior surface of the closed wings as well. When we look at the altar in Isenheim when closed, we gaze upon the tragic figure of Christ. He hangs on a rough-hewn cross silhouetted against the darkened sky. The artist has caught the supreme agony of the event in the figure of the Christ and in the faces of the crowd who scorned him. On holy days, however, the altar is opened—and here the artist has pictured a divine miracle. The scenes are not of earth but of heaven. Instead of the darkness of Calvary there is the golden light of the celestial city; in place of the hostile crowd there are shining angels. The artist has visioned the glory of heaven as immediately behind the cross.

G. ERNEST THOMAS

250. EVENSONG

What tender, trustful, triumphant words they were, breathing a prayer of peace after the storm: "Into Thy hands I commit my spirit." Someone has pointed out that this was the bedside prayer which every Hebrew mother taught her child as the evening shadows fell —like the little prayers we learned long ago, and have taught to our children; and so the first faith of Jesus was the last, as befitted One to whom the child-heart was the finest flower and essence of religion. Nothing is easier than to keep our first faith when the sky is sunny overhead and the path smooth before us. But when shadows fall, and the storms beat upon us, it is different. The ministry of Jesus in Galilee was like a summer; but in Judea He met icy hostility, cold indifference, trickery among His enemies and treachery among His friends, "and it was winter." Yet through all trial, all temptation, all tragedy, up to the last bitter hour, He kept the highest and sweetest faith. Thus the evensong which His mother had taught Him long ago lingered last upon His lips, as He entered "the deep, vast, speechlessness of death."

JOSEPH FORT NEWTON

D. THE NINTH HOUR

251. EMPHASIS ON HIS DEATH

The space which the Four Gospels give to the death of Christ is very striking. Two of the Gospels do not relate the birth of Jesus; two do not relate his temptation; two of them have no record of the Sermon on the Mount; two of them have no account of his ascension into heaven; but all relate with fullness of detail the story of his crucifixion and death. One-third of Matthew, one-third of Mark, and one-fourth of Luke is devoted to the account of Christ's death, and one-half of John's Gospel to the last twenty-four hours of Christ's life. One-third of the material in the Four Gospels has to do with the events of the last week of the life of Jesus. If the death of Christ was given such an amount of space by these four authors—two of them apostles, and two of them (Mark and Luke) in touch with the apostles—the only explanation is that Christ himself, by his words and his death, made that impression upon them.

This prominence given to the death of Jesus in the biographies of the Four Gospels is in strange contrast with the biographies of the notable men of history. In a recent biography of Daniel Webster, just five of the 863 pages which deal with the life of the great statesman and orator tell of his death at Marshfield. In *Abraham Lincoln, A Biography,* by Nicolay and Hay, there are 5,000 pages, and just 25 of these pages relate the dramatic story of Lincoln's assassination and death. In a recent life of the poet Shelley, just three pages out of 1,389 pages tell the sad story of Shelley's death by drowning near Leghorn in 1822.

CLARENCE E. MACARTNEY

252. GREAT UNEXPLORED WORLD

The death of Jesus has been the subject of more thought, one can say without exaggeration, than anything that has occupied the mind of

113

man. No treatment of it ever satisfies listener or reader as complete or adequate; the best gives one the sense of having touched, as it were, the mere hem of the garment. Whenever we look at him, and think again of his death with any firmness and reality, most of our previous thought seems to be of little consequence, and we are left with the feeling of a great unexplored world before us, of more beyond. In this it resembles the great things of Nature, which are never exhausted, which always have mystery and wonder and happiness in reserve. A man who supposes that he can speak with any adequacy of the death of Jesus is simply not thinking about it at all. But the very difficulty of the subject and the failure of attempts to deal with it are compulsive reasons for studying it. It is too central, too vital, to go unstudied. Better to fail than not to attempt it, for failure will at least reveal something of the greatness of the subject.

T. R. GLOVER

253. CONSUMMATION OF HIS WORK

It is hardly necessary to prove that in the New Testament the death of Christ is a real subject. It is distinctly present to the mind of New Testament writers, and they have much to say upon it. It is treated by them as a subject of central and permanent importance to the Christian faith, and it is incredible that it should have filled the place it does fill in the New Testament had it ever been regarded as of trifling consequence for the understanding, the acceptance, or the preaching of the Gospel. It is hardly necessary to say that in using the expression "the death of Christ," we are not speaking of a thing, but of an experience. Whether we view it as action or as passion, whatever enters into personality has the significance and the worth of personality. The death of Christ in the New Testament is the death of one who is alive for evermore. To every New Testament writer Christ is the Lord, the living and exalted Lord, and it is impossible for them to think of His death except as an experience the result or virtue of which is perpetuated in His risen life. Nevertheless, Christ died. His death is in some sense the centre and consummation of His work. It is because of it that His risen life is the hope which it is to sinful men; and it needs no apology, therefore, if one who thinks that it has less than its proper place in preaching and in theology

114

endeavours to bring out as simply as possible its place and meaning in the New Testament. If our religion is to be Christian in any sense of the term which history will justify, it can never afford to ignore what, to say the least of it, is the primary confession of Christian faith.

JAMES DENNEY. .

254. NO LONGER SEPARATED

"The curtain of the temple was torn in two." The temple tore its gown as the mourners did because He, to whom the temple belonged more than to anybody else, was thrown out and killed by the servants of the temple. But the temple—and with it, all temples on earth—also complained of its own destiny. The curtain which made the temple a holy place, separated from other places, lost its separating power. He who was expelled as blaspheming the temple, had cleft the curtain and opened the temple for everybody, for every moment. *This* curtain cannot be mended any more, although there are priests and ministers and pious people who try to mend it. They will *not* succeed because He, for whom every place was a sacred place, a place where God is present, has been brought on the Cross in the name of the holy place. When the curtain of the temple was torn in two, God judged religion and rejected temples. After this moment temples and churches can only mean place of concentration on the holy which is the ground and meaning of every place.

PAUL TILLICH

255. *FROM* EASTER EVEN

There is nothing more that they can do
    For all their rage and boast:
Caiaphas with his blaspheming crew,
    Herod with his host;

Pontius Pilate in his judgmenthall
    Judging their Judge and his,
Or he who led them all and passed them all,
    Arch-Judas with his kiss.

115

The sepulchre made sure with ponderous stone,
　Seal that same stone, O priest:
It may be thou shalt block the Holy One
　From rising in the east.

Set a watch about the sepulchre
　To watch on pain of death:
They must hold fast the stone if One should stir
　And shake it from beneath.

Christina G. Rossetti

256. AFTER CALVARY

For Martha, there were dishes
To be washed ere close of day,
Matzoths to bake for breakfast,
And crumbs to sweep away.
For Martha, there was dust-fluff,
The board to set; a broom—
That kept her mind away from
One hanging in the gloom.

For Mary, there was twilight
And one star that kissed a hill;
For her were trees and springtime
Beyond her windowsill.
For Mary, there were shadows,
A lily's breath, a leaf—
That tore her heart with pity
And nailed her soul with grief.

Violet Alleyn Storey

E. WERE YOU THERE?

257. I WAS THERE

Were you there when they crucified my Lord? I was there. I can see
myself in each of the actors in that drama. I was there in Caiaphas

who would save the nation by letting Jesus perish. I was there in Nicodemus who would not risk his position in the Sanhedrin for Jesus' sake. I was there in Peter who loved but was unprepared. I was there in Judas who followed, but sought to bend Jesus to his own ends. I was there in Herod who did not care. I was there in Pilate who was afraid. I was there among the fickle crowd. I was one of the soldiers who simply did his duty. I know I am guilty of his death.

DANIEL T. NILES

258. NO REASON FOR CONCERN

Would we have been with Caiaphas, defending the faith of our fathers against this radical innovator and blasphemer? Would we have stood with Pilate, approving the crucifixion of this rebellious Jew in the interests of the peace and order of the empire? Presumably we would not have been associated with Herod in his complete self-regard and sadistic inclinations. But might we not have been like the soldiers, finding ourselves in an official position and simply obeying the orders of our superiors? Surely we would not have been with the mob, voicing its sadism in the cry, "Crucify him." Is it not likely, however, that we might easily have been among those who had paid no attention to Jesus in his lifetime and now saw no reason to be concerned? Or among those who had openly or secretly admired Jesus and perhaps been helped by him, but who, under the influence of natural human fear, had taken an attitude of indifference and inertia, and said, "I don't want to get mixed up in anything that is not my business."

GARDINER M. DAY

259. WE ARE INVOLVED

Recall that moving Negro spiritual, "When they crucified my Lord, were you there?" Even to ask that question is strange. Suppose it concerned the slaying of Julius Caesar. That, too, was a momentous tragedy yet who ever thought of asking whether we were there? But this other question is asked and has been asked in manifold ways times without number across the centuries: "When they crucified my Lord, were you there?" Well, we were there; in a deep sense we are

117

there. All the major factors in that tragedy involve you and me. The blindness of religious leaders who cannot see a new and larger truth, the selfishness of a business community that does not want the profitable traffic in the temple courts disturbed, the disloyalty of Judas, who cares more for himself than for Christ, the political shrewdness of Pilate, who does his best to free Jesus, but, finding it costs too much, washes his hands of it, the emotionalism of the crowd, stirred by effective propaganda to cry for they know not what, the fearfulness of disciples who run away—who of us was not there?

Not one unusual sin was involved in the crucifixion of Jesus. Say, as we will, that the tragic result was the towering crime of history, doing to a shameful death the "young Prince of Glory," still it was our small, familiar, day-by-day sins that did it. I have walked the streets of Jerusalem and recapitulated in detail the events of that last week, and alas, how easy for one to imagine oneself sharing in it all! When they crucified our Lord, we were there.

Harry Emerson Fosdick

260. THE INWARD CROSS

With the death of Jesus, the drama of the cross did not end, but its stage was changed. It was moved from the geographical site of Calvary, a small hill outside Jerusalem, to the heart of every man, woman, or child who seeks to understand the meaning of his own life and to clarify his relationships with other people on the most realistic level.

The cross was outward on the original Good Friday. It stood over against the men who saw it, outside their lives, something to which they were related only as spectators. With the death of Jesus in the spirit of confident victory, the cross was made inward for every man, woman, and child who is discontent with being a spectator in the game of life, and would participate in honesty and truth.

When you and I, as the drama of Calvary is played to the conclusion, contemplate the cross, we see either the stark evidence of a tragedy that is over or we see the creative symbol of a new power and vision in which we can share. If we see only an outward cross, we see only the former; but if the cross has become an inward reality in our own hearts, then we see the latter, not just in theory but in fact.

The inward cross means that I am a new man, living in a new

118

world, because Jesus Christ died for me that I might live today by his spirit, related to my brethren by a common faith built upon his foundation. It means that I am ready to accept death as the measure of life, going ahead with confidence in the purpose of God, provided I share the humility of the cross. It means that this tortured world in which I live has a hope that cannot be betrayed, if once it is understood for what it is meant to be. It means that you and I may live now by triumphant faith.

Charles Duell Kean

F. WHY JESUS DIED

261. FIVE INTERPRETATIONS

Christ died (1) because under the conditions of the time it was inevitable—as it had been inevitable (historically) that John the Baptist and other martyrs should die. Not only because tyrants now governed the nation, but because men are what they are. "It is impossible that a prophet should perish away from Jerusalem" (Luke 13:33). He died (2) because in a world like this, which always destroys its best—it unfailingly does so in its wars—the political, social, religious conditions always continue to make Christ a martyr and lead to the murder of the prophets. He died (3) because it was so written in the Scriptures, in Isaiah 53, in Psalm 22, and elsewhere—the Scriptures themselves reflecting, and in a measure interpreting, this fatal trait in human nature and in the world's history. He died (4) because God permitted it; and since God is absolutely sovereign, He must will what He permits. God's purpose is evident from the later consequences, the removal of sin, the breaking down of the barrier between Himself and the world, the whole new life in grace, the new creation, the new "being" in Christ. Finally, he died (5) because he himself willed to die—in taking the risk involved in going to Jerusalem, of which anyone could have warned him. This was not suicide, but the acceptance of God's way for him to go. And out of it came, and have ever come, the blessings of a new life for all who accept his way, take up his cross, and live in him.

Frederick C. Grant

262. WHAT CRUCIFIED CHRIST?

It is not enough to possess abundant life; that abundant life must be witnessed to and lived out in the presence of some Pontius Pilate—something that stands athwart this new life, and to meet it unflinchingly means that this new life will crimson into a cross. This business of being Christian in a world of this kind is no easy undertaking. We have to meet the equivalent of Pilate. And that would mean?

To discover its meaning we must ask, not *who* crucified Christ, but *what?* For the who embodied a what. Seven embodied sins combined to crucify Jesus. (1) Self-interested moral cowardice—Pilate. (2) Vested class interests—the priests. (3) Envy—the priests. (4) Faithless friendships—Judas. (5) Ignorance—the multitude. (6) Indifference—the multitude. (7) Race-prejudiced militarism—the Roman soldiers.

E. Stanley Jones

263. LOVE FOR THEIR SAKE

How Christ's death takes away thy sins thou wilt never know on earth—perhaps not in heaven. It is a mystery which thou must believe and adore. But *why* He died thou canst see at the first glance, if thou hast a human heart and will look at what God means thee to look at—Christ upon His Cross. He died because He was *Love*— love itself, love boundless, unconquerable, unchangeable—love which inhabits eternity, and therefore could not be hardened or foiled by any sin or rebellion of man, but must love men still—must go out to seek and save them, must dare, suffer any misery, shame, death itself, for their sake—just because it is absolute and perfect Love which inhabits eternity.

Charles Kingsley

264. THREAT OF TRUTH

The Christ was not crucified by criminals or by men who fell below the ordinary standards of human virtue. Such criminals were crucified with Christ. One of the instruments of crucifixion was the Roman system of jurisprudence which rightly boasted the highest achievements of justice in the ancient world. But even a boasted system of impartial justice is sufficiently human to fear that its majesty may be challenged by one who proclaimed himself a king. The kingdom of truth is a threat to every historical majesty. Every historical majesty is more anxious and insecure than it pretends. A priestly oligarchy was also implicated in the crucifixion. This oligarchy was certain that it was merely defending a very sublime system of religious legalism against an impious rebel; but it was also defending its moral prestige and its security. That is the fate of all historic oligarchies and institutions. There is always an anxious life, individuals or collective, behind the most imposing facade of ideals and principles, of values and eternal verities, to the defense of which men rise in history.

REINHOLD NIEBUHR

265. WHAT HE MIGHT HAVE DONE

He might have compromised with the priests—made a bargain with Caiaphas, talked things over with Pilate.

He might have made His kingdom political instead of spiritual. He might have chosen the expedient rather than the right.

As He Himself reminded Peter, He might have called upon twelve legions of angels to rescue Him and show His great power.

He might have withstood the plottings and devices of wicked men. Yes, He might have saved Himself. He had the power; but then He would never have been our Saviour!
For no man can save himself who saves another.

If any man will save others, in any salvation whatsoever, the mandate he must obey,
   the stern condition he must fulfill,
is that he cannot save himself.
Such is the paradox of salvation!

The acorn cannot save itself, if it is to bud a tree.
The soldier cannot save himself, if he is to save his country.

121

Nor can the Shepherd save Himself, if He would save His sheep. Christ is the Good Shepherd, and hence, when He would consummate the great salvation, there was no other way to save us than to lay down His life for our salvation.

For to love is never to think of one's self, but to give one's self for the one loved.

And He loved us and gave Himself for us.

PETER MARSHALL

266. HE DIED FOR PEOPLE

Precisely because he would save others he could not save himself. He died for a cause, a vision, an ideal. Others have done no less, it is said; Jesus is not unique in having done this. That is perfectly true, and far from detracting from the wonder, and the specifically unique quality about the sacrifice of Christ, this fact should make us all the more sensible of how much we owe to those of former ages, and of our own, who have given themselves in order that we might have life at its fullest and best.

Some there are who would repudiate this vehemently. "I refuse to accept the claim that Christ died for me," such a one declares. "How could a first-century Jew, however good a man he was, die for a twentieth-century man?" "What possible effect can that one far-off death long ago have upon me here and now?" But the more vehemently the protest is made, the more uneasy, one feels, the protestant is. Whether we like it and accept it, or not, Christ did die for us all. Moreover, neither can we cut our selves off from our inheritance, and we are the heirs of many ages. The sacrifices and sufferings of that long line of our forebears must lay a moral compulsion upon us when we truly reflect upon them.

Christ did not die so much for a cause, a vision, an ideal, as for men and women, individuals, human souls, that they might be brought back from their wanderings and their estrangement, from their follies, failures, and sins, home to their Father God. Although now a man may well refuse to accept this, indignantly repudiating the very idea of it, perhaps because he has heard or read some atone-

ment theory that he cannot stomach, for it offends his sense of justice
—and some good men have turned from God because they have felt
that he has been shown to be less just than his creation—the day will
yet come when that man will have his eyes opened, and he will know
it to be very truth that Christ did die for him.

John Trevor Davies

G. GOD WAS IN CHRIST

267. THE FATHER GRIEVES

An impressive picture of Calvary can be seen in the National Gallery
in London. Christ is on the cross, almost hidden in the darkness. At
first the one who looks observes nothing in the blackness and through
it the dim figure of the suffering Christ. But if his gaze does not
falter, he glimpses a figure with arms outstretched, tenderly holding
up the suffering one. His face is twisted by a pain which is more
agonizing even than that of Christ. God the Father is grieving with
his Son as he hangs on the cross.

G. Ernest Thomas

268. WAY OF OBEDIENCE

Christ pursued his way of sacrifice unto death in obedience to the will
of God. It was God's will that suffering and death should strike him.
He not only suffered himself; God gave him as a sacrifice. God "gave"
him not only by sending him into the world but also by sending him
to death. From one point of view his suffering and death were a
result of the attack by the hostile powers on him. But from a more
serious point of view this was a case of divine necessity. It was God's
will that this evil should strike him. His enemies did not offer him;
they only did violence to him. We would not express the whole
truth if we said that God simply "permitted" him to be put to death.
He gave himself, and God gave him as a sacrifice.

Gustaf Aulén

269. GOD'S DEVOTION

We never understand the meaning of the cross for God unless we recall what is implied in John's description of His character: "God is love." Then Calvary becomes inevitable from all eternity. From the moment when God gave another being life, His parental responsibility required Him to devote Himself to that other's perfecting. If His child sinned, He must suffer with and for him, and He cannot cease loving him, nor doing for him all that love endlessly suggests. The Lamb was slain in the conscience of God from the foundation of the world. From the moment there was a world for which God was accountable, He could not withhold His nearest and dearest, He could not spare Himself. He was a debtor to all on whom He had brought the miseries and exposed to the temptations of life, so as much as in Him lay He was ready to serve them. Calvary is the typical event in time through which we look in on God's eternal self-devotion to His children.

HENRY SLOANE COFFIN

270. I SAW GOD BARE HIS SOUL ONE DAY

I saw God bare his soul one day
    Where all the earth might see
The stark and naked heart of him
    On lonely Calvary.

There was a crimson sky of blood
    And overhead a storm;
When lightning slit the clouds
    And light engulfed his form.

Beyond the storm a rainbow lent
    A light to every clod,
And on that cross mine eyes beheld
    The naked soul of God.

WILLIAM L. STIDGER

271. SUFFERING LOVE

To-day the most significant aspect which we find for our time in the Cross of Christ is its identification with and its revelation of *the*

124

suffering love of God as Father. It seems to me as I study the story— "the good news"—which Christ's life presents, this aspect of His mission stands out in clear relief from the beginning to the end of the story. The unique feature everywhere in evidence in the experience of Christ is the marvelous comprehension, in fact the actual experience, of the love and tenderness of God as Father. Love of that sort, from the nature of the case, could never "run smooth" in a world where there was sin and blunder and imperfection. The "Law" had met the situation by thinking of God as Sovereign and by pointing out the way in which God's divine rights and His sovereign justice could be met and satisfied. But Christ divinely leaped to a wholly new interpretation of God. His nature, His character, for Christ, is essentially that of tender, loving Father. He does not *become* loving, as a result of human efforts to satify Him. He does not *cease* to be loving, through man's blunder, sin and failure. He simply *is* Father, eternally and unalterably Father. That means essentially that grace and not justice, is the deepest fact there is about God—and grace is love, spontaneous, uncalculating, going the whole way through, never letting go, never despairing, never losing patience, and suffering as one must suffer when the person who is loved goes wrong. Christ is this amazing grace of God made vocal and incarnate.

RUFUS M. JONES

272. DIVINE AND HUMAN TRAGEDY

In Marie Augustin Zwiller's picture "The First Night Outside Paradise" Adam and Eve have been driven from Eden, and we see them looking back toward it. An angel with a flaming sword guards the gate. They are not looking, however, at the angel. Their eyes are lifted above him; for there, illuminating the darkening sky, is the bright outline of a Cross; and they are gazing wonderingly at that. The picture portrays the tremendous fact that God is of such a nature that he must be concerned with every crisis of human life and involved in every moment of human tragedy. Because the very nature of ultimate reality is good, human tragedy involves divine tragedy, so that with the birth of human need was born divine salvation.

ERNEST WALL

VII. Measure of the Cross

A. SOVEREIGN EMBLEM

273. *FROM* THE CATHEDRAL

The Cross, bold type of shame to homage turned,
Of an unfinished life that sways the world,
Shall tower as sovereign emblem over all.

JAMES RUSSELL LOWELL

274. AT THE CENTER OF FAITH

The cross stands at the center of the Christian religion. No other symbol adopted during the centuries of his historical existence can compare in importance with the cross. It is the dominating theme in art and architecture, it is the determinative criterion in faith and conduct, it is the impelling motive in devotion and service. Other systems revolve around other symbols—the crescent, the sickle, the lotus flower, the spinning wheel, the sun's disk, the living flame—but Christianity revolves around the cross. Nothing has a right to the name "Christian" that is contrary to or incompatible with all that this symbol represents.

F. W. DILLISTONE

275. INDISPENSABLE SYMBOL

Throughout this kaleidoscopic history of two thousand years Christianity's symbol has remained a cross. The fact seems to be that mankind feels this symbol to be indispensable. Why this should be so is not easy to account for. One would think that its symbol might have been an empty tomb, or a great cathedral, or a figure of the compassionate one. Yet there never seems to have been a question that the Cross should not be its only possible symbol. The multitudes of good men who have given their allegiance to Christianity in one way or another have sensed that the Cross says something about life which nothing else could do. The Cross has a relevance to the lives of good men through which the nature of life is revealed with peculiar and incisive accuracy. Its power is remarkable for this very reason, that makes its irresistible impression upon the minds and hearts of those who, in their time, are considered the good men. The Cross more than anything else has had something to say to those who presumably do not have to have anything said to them.

JOHN C. SCHROEDER

276. MORE THAN SENTIMENT

The Cross was an open secret to the first disciples, and they climbed the steep ascent to Heaven by the "Royal Way of the Holy Cross," but its simplicity has been often veiled in later days. Perhaps the simplicity of the symbol has cast a glamour over the modern mind and blinded us to its strenuous meaning. Art, for instance, with an unerring instinct of moral beauty, has seized the Cross and idealised it. It is wrought in gold and hung from the neck of light-hearted beauty; it is stamped on the costly binding of Bibles that go to church in carriages; it stands out in bold relief on churches that are filled with easy-going people. Painters have given themselves to crucifixions, and their striking works are criticised by persons who praise the thorns in the crown, but are not quite pleased with the expression on Jesus' face, and then returned to their pleasures. Composers have cast the bitter Passion of Jesus into stately oratorios, and fashionable audiences are affected unto tears. Jesus' Cross has been taken out of His hands and smothered with flowers: it has become what He would have hated, a source of graceful ideas and agreeable emotions. When Jesus presented the Cross for the salvation of His disciples, He was certainly not thinking of a sentiment, which can disturb no man's life, nor redeem any man's soul, but of the unsightly beam which must be set up in the midst of a man's pleasures, and the jagged nails that must pierce his soul.

JOHN WATSON

B. CROSS AND SUFFERING

277. FACT OF SUFFERING

It is with the holiest fear that we should approach the terrible fact of the sufferings of our Lord. Let no one think that these were less because He was more. The more delicate the nature, the more alive to all that is lovely and true, lawful and right, the more does it feel the antagonism of pain, the inroad of death upon life; the more dreadful is that breach of the harmony of things whose sound is torture.

GEORGE MACDONALD

278. HE KNEW SUFFERING

Of all men Christ had most right to speak about suffering. That is why we are bound to listen to him and take his guiding. He knew the last thing about it. He knew suffering at its most poignant level in every known form. Even before he came to the Cross he had had much experience of it. He had known bitter disappointment, unpopularity, misunderstanding, the disloyalty of friends, as well as the pain that comes through the vital sympathy in which he was so fully one with his fellows. It all culminated on Calvary. We cannot even imagine the agony of physical crucifixion. The mind reels at the outrageous cruelty of it. But that was not all. There was the scorn, the contempt, the misunderstanding of the world. When we suffer pain we are surrounded by sympathetic friends supporting us with their loyalty. But think of that death scene on Calvary, his utter loneliness, the sounds he heard in the strange silence that fell—curses, sneers, laughter, mockery; and to his sensitive mind a loveless word was a blow. To add to its bitterness it was his own people who were crucifying him—the people he had given everything he had to help and save. No one can doubt that he entered into all our human experience of suffering.

. . JAMES REID

279. HIS SPIRITUAL DEATH

The physical suffering of Jesus Christ was not the real suffering. Many men before Him had died. Many men had become martyrs. The awful suffering of Jesus Christ was His spiritual death. He reached the final issue of sin, fathomed the deepest sorrow, when God turned His back and hid His face so that He cried, "My God, why hast Thou forsaken me?" Alone in the supreme hour of mankind's history Christ uttered these words! Light blazed forth to give us a glimpse of what He was enduring, but the light was so blinding, as G. Campbell Morgan says, "that no eye could bear to gaze." The words were uttered, as Dr. Morgan has so well expressed it, "that man may know how much there is that may not be known."

He who knew no sin was made to be sin on our behalf that we might become the righteousness of God in Him. On the cross He was made sin. He was God-forsaken. Because He knew no sin there is a value beyond comprehension in the penalty He bore, a penalty that He did not need for Himself. If in bearing sin in His own body He created a value that He did not need for Himself, for whom was the value created?

How it was accomplished in the depth of the darkness man will never know. I know only one thing—He bore my sins in His body upon the tree. He stood where I should have stood. The pains of hell that were my portion were heaped on Him, and I am able to go to heaven and merit that which is not my own, but is His by every right.

BILLY GRAHAM

280. WITH AND FOR MAN

Suffering, if it is self-enclosed, all dammed up within the soul, may indeed become a poison to the soul. There is no gospel in such affliction, no gospel in mere suffering for the sake of suffering. But again, with Paul, if we suffer with God then pain becomes for us what it was for Christ: a way into the heart of God's family. Through my pain I can take my stand beside pain-filled hearts in all the places of the earth. On the cross Christ endured pain, not just for himself; he suffered there *with* and *for* all men. We speak altogether too casually about "bearing our crosses." Sometimes we make it seem

129

almost as though minor inconveniences to our comfort had become crosses. Notwithstanding, in a profound way suffering can become for us a cross if we accept it with God, and if it leads us to suffer with all men as Christ was doing on the cross.

ROBERT E. LUCCOCK

281. VICARIOUS SUFFERING

Forgiveness is an immediate personal relation which restores a broken fellowship. Even though the guilt is forgiven the consequences of sin still go on. Forgiveness does not mean escape from punishment. Vicarious punishment means the sharing of punishment both on the personal and on the natural level. In Gethsemane Jesus suffered vicariously on the personal level; on Calvary, on the natural level as well. It is not only that in this life we pay the consequences of our sins and that in the next we shall receive rewards or punishment in our bodies according to our deeds. The forgiven murderer may still be hanged. The saint who had a sexual lapse may not only suffer himself, though forgiven, but cause much suffering to others. There is a grand majesty in the moral life. Even in the spiritual life where forgiveness is immediate and direct, God's grace increases our sufferings. The more we partake of God's love the more we feel the sins and sorrows of the world. The deeper our experience of forgiveness, the more we suffer vicariously. The closer we live to the Cross of Christ the more we share his redemptive passion. Forgiveness involves taking up our crosses to follow Christ. It endows us with the suffering love without which we cannot be ambassadors of Christ, and as Luther put it, saviors to others.

NELS F. S. FERRÉ

282. ROAD TO VICTORY

The suffering God is not simply the teaching of modern divines, it is a New Testament thought, and it is one that answers all the doubts that arise at the sight of human suffering. To know that God is suffering with it makes that suffering more awful; but it gives *strength* and *life* and *hope,* for we know that if God is in it, suffering is the *road to victory!* If He share our suffering, we shall share His crown.

ALEXANDRE VINET

283. TAKEN IN STRIDE

The Savior of the world was no ascetic, no dream-haunted absentee from paths that we poor folk must tread. He passed our way and found it rougher than we do. His lesson is, not how to die, but how to live that death may be but the gate that opens into a fuller life. Hunger and thirst had been His portion when the Son of Man had not where to lay His head. Only these things were not suffered to hold Him back from the Father's business. He took them in His stride, but owned that they hurt. He never went around His trials, but through them, and there is all the difference in the world between the two methods of meeting suffering. When He suffered and said that He suffered, He did not pray for miraculous deliverance, but out of the grandeur of His own soul, and with the assistance of a friend, He dealt with the lesser evil of pain that had come to Him as He pursued the Father's way.

DICK SHEPPARD

284. VIA DOLOROSA

Devout Christians have paid in the coin of suffering for their fellowship with Christ. Tradition holds that Peter was crucified. John the Baptist was imprisoned and beheaded. Stephen was stoned to death, and Paul suffered the lash and the headsman's ax. Other Christians were driven to the catacombs, thrown into the arena, lighted as human torches. Bunyan, Tyndale, Latimer, Knox, and a host of others, in their fellowship with Christ, found suffering in their conquest of an ignorant, wicked, and cruel world.

Modes of torture may have changed, but anyone who dares to be definitely Christian today will suffer some form of crucifixion. If he escapes a concentration camp, he will be maligned, scoffed at, or ostracized. Moreover, who dares say that it is easy to know what is right, to do what is right, to return good for evil, to bless them who

131

practice selfishness and abuse? What beds of ease can a Christian now find in subterranean shelter? What pleasure can he have from the alkaline taste of the ashes falling in the world conflagration? From the point of view of physical torture and mental agony, the road a true Christian must travel is indeed the *via dolorosa*.

A. C. REID

C. CROSS AND SIN

285. THE CROSS MADE NECESSARY

The entire New New Testament connects the Cross with man's sin. It was the reality of sin which made the Cross "necessary" in the working out of God's purpose in history. For early Christians the Crucifixion-Resurrection was the revelation of God's initiative, his willingness to do for man what he could not do for himself. In this way his forgiveness intersected the self-centered circle of man's existence. The Cross, therefore, was no mere accidental development in history; it was a necessary part of God's redemptive plan (Acts 2:23). Jesus' death was not the death of an ordinary martyr. God himself was identified with the event. He was "in Christ." His forgiveness was "made flesh." He had stepped across the chasm of man's sin and had manifested his sovereign power.

BERNHARD W. ANDERSON

286. CHARACTER OF EVIL

One reason why the Cross of Christ has so wrought on the consciences of men is that it exhibits the true character of moral evil by expressing it in terms of suffering, which all can understand. The sins of men actually crucified Jesus—the sins of the Jewish Sanhedrin, which were jealousy and prejudice, the sin of Judas who betrayed Him, the sin of Peter who denied Him, the sin of Pontius Pilate, who found injustice easier than justice, the sin of Roman soldiers, who added mocking to His scourging and crucifixion. These are *our* sins as much as theirs—jealousy, prejudice, disloyalty, time-serving, pitilessness—though the consequences are not so clearly seen, when *we* are the sinners. Yet, in similar circumstances, without the light that history has flung upon the Cross, any of us might do like deeds. But just because the result of those ancient sins is revealed in the suffering of the Cross, we are made to see what sin really is. Sin is something that can do things like *that*.

H. Wheeler Robinson

287. CHRIST THEIR SUBSTITUTE

At the foot of Christ's cross, men have known a conscience of sin, a horror of it, and by consequence, a penitence for their own share in it, deeper than anything else has started in human experience. And as thus their whole spiritual nature has been aroused, and they have awakened to the truth that it would not have been safe, nor in any wise morally well, for them to have been forgiven by mere clemency and without feeling what sin costs, they come to understand that in His sufferings Christ was their substitute.

George Adam Smith

288. MORAL DYNAMIC

If men are to be effectually brought to repentance and reconciled to God, these things at least need to be stabbed into their consciousness: the moral loathsomeness of sin; the Divine holiness that inevitably condemns it; the outreaching Love that forgives it and restores; and the perfect human obedience that has been and can be rendered. The Cross of Christ is unique as a moral dynamic because it fills all these needs.

Edward Grubb

289. SIGN OF RESCUE

He died for sinners, according to His own word; and ever since, His cross has been the sign of rescue for humanity. Whatever may be the nature of that sublime transaction upon Calvary; whatever the name by which men call it,—Atonement, Sacrifice, Redemption, Propitiation; whatever relations it may have to the eternal moral law and to the Divine righteousness,—its relation to the human heart is luminous and beautiful. It does take away sin. Kneeling at that holy altar, the soul at once remembers most vividly, and confesses most humbly, and loses most entirely, all her guilt. A sense of profound, unutterable relief, a sacred quietude, diffuses itself through all the recesses of the troubled spirit. Looking unto Christ crucified, we receive an assurance of sin forgiven, which goes deeper than thought can fathom, and far deeper than words can measure.

HENRY VAN DYKE

290. PRAYER ON GOOD FRIDAY

Blood of Jesus, shed for me,
Cleanse my sin and make me free.

Let His life, so freely given,
Heal our world asunder riven.

Let His words of love and peace
Rule our lives till strife shall cease.

Let His faith, His grace and power,
Be our strength in this dark hour.

Cross of Christ, undimmed by wrong,
Be today my triumph song!

GEORGIA HARKNESS

D. DOCTRINE OF ATONEMENT

291. IF WE WERE ABLER

We often speak of the mystery of the Atonement . . . and often by our very manner of saying this, a suggestion is left that the difficulties are purely intellectual. If we were abler, if our minds were more subtle or profound, it is hinted, we should not find the Cross so unfathomable as we do. But doesn't the difficulty lie far, far deeper? I feel that the great reason why we fail to understand Calvary is not merely that we are not profound enough, it is that we are not good enough. It is because we are such strangers to sacrifice that God's sacrifice leaves us bewildered. It is because we love so little that His love is mysterious. We have never forgiven anybody at such a cost as His. We have never taken the initiative in putting a quarrel right with His kind of unreserved willingness to suffer. It is our unlikeness to God that hangs as an obscuring screen impeding our view, and we see the Atonement so often through the frosted glass of our own lovelessness.

H. R. MACKINTOSH

292. ESSENCE OF ATONEMENT

The eternal love of God suffering the *necessary reaction* of His own holiness against the sin of His creatures *and with a view to their salvation*—this is the essence of the atonement.

AUGUSTUS H. STRONG

293. ALREADY WON

God Himself, in the person of Christ the Son, has satisfied His own claims upon us. When Christ died on Calvary, the sacrifice we could not offer was offered for us, the debt we could not pay was paid for us—both figures have had large place in the history of Christian thought. The Christian good news is that all that is demanded of us has already been accomplished for us—was for ever accomplished when Jesus Christ, as He died, said, "It is finished." Our salvation is already secured. It is there for us to take. We must not try to win it; all we need do is to receive it. Or again, as the New Testament so often expresses it, all we need do is to *believe* it—to believe that it has already been won. Salvation, we are told, is not by works but by faith.

JOHN BAILLIE

294. THEORIES OF THE CROSS

If His Cross were only the story of a man, hanging on a crossbeam of wood, giving his life for what he deeply believed, any good newspaper reporter could tell that story in a few paragraphs. However, the finest of Christian scholarship, the best of Christian experience and the truest of Christian insight for twenty centuries have not been able to fathom the depths of the Cross. In an effort to do so great scholars and saints of the Church have developed at least five theories of what Jesus did on His Cross. There is mighty truth in each of them and material to illustrate or substantiate each of them is found in this Gospel.

First, there is the *Ransom Theory*. Jesus gave "His life a ransom for many." Never mind to whom the ransom was paid, the real question is whether we for whom He died are still of sin the slaves? Are we free men?

There is no doubt that He set the praying, penitent thief free. The thief only asked to be "remembered" but Jesus gave him more than he asked for. Jesus assured the poor fellow that he would be "with him." To know Christ's living presence, His resources, guidance and companionship under any and all circumstances, anywhere and everywhere—that is the greatest, if not the only, security and freedom this earth knows. Standing fast in the liberty wherewith Christ has set us free means to get from this living presence of Jesus the power to do what we ought to do. Freedom is not the right to do what one pleases—that pretty generally means slavery of some kind. Freedom, on the other hand, means achievement. Away, then, with old habits that enslave! Away with the demand for selfish rights. . . . A free man is one who is ready to be and capable of being the free instrument of the Eternal—the mind, the heart, the life through which Christ can think, love and act. That means to possess His living presence. "Today shalt thou be with me." To be thus set free is to be "ransomed" indeed.

Second, there is the *Governmental Theory*. Interesting that this conception should have been propounded by the founder of international law! Nothing so interferes with the government and life of men as the presence of evil in personal life and social relationships. And no other person in human history has handled this power of evil as has Jesus. It is His greatest gift to men. He is the first of earth's great not alone because of His own personal perfection but because of what He can do to handle the power and presence of evil in every man's life. But, take His Cross away from Him, and this gift of handling sin is weakened if not removed. The Cross is His instrument. Indeed, He rules from the Cross. The Cross literally decreases the amount of evil in the world and makes human government of men more possible. The obvious need for this in our day is writ large across the face of the whole earth. . . .

Third, there is the *Moral Influence Theory*. The Cross speaks in words like these: Look what love will do for what it believes and for whom it loves. So the Cross calls men to enlarge their "beliefs" and "loves." Remember what Jesus said on that Cross and consider the moral influence of His example. . . . Nothing short of a Christ who set the example of suffering as the Christian way of dealing with human problems would inspire men to suffer for what they believe. . . .

Fourth, there is the *Substitutionary Theory*. His critics out front on the Day of the Cross cried, "If thou be the king of the Jews, save thyself." But Jesus couldn't save Himself and us.

To make this matter crystal clear, let's try to put ourselves into the shoes or sandals of one man who will never forget that day. That man is Barabbas. He was the man previously condemned to die but the people elected Jesus to the Cross in His place. Indeed, God Himself had appointed Jesus. Some cruel, brutal, seemingly unfair things that men do seem to be under the control of a mighty move of the Eternal like the tide of the sea.

Surely Barabbas was standing there, near the Cross, constantly saying to himself, "He died for me. . . . He is taking my place." That is the way every penitent heart must feel. Jesus set Barabbas free by taking his place. He sets us free by taking ours.

Fifth, there is the *Reconciliation Theory*. "God was in Christ, reconciling the world until himself." Men everywhere were prodigals. They had wandered far from the Father's heart and purpose. Sin had come between them and His fellowship.

So Jesus announced, "And I, if I be lifted up from the earth will draw all men unto me." The Cross was the magnet by which God drew men back to His fellowship and purpose. And now, let's change the tense. It is not past but present. Jesus draws men to Himself through the pulling power of the Cross and so reconciles men and God. God never needed to be reconciled. He loves men forever. Man is the prodigal and the Cross draws him back to the Father's heart.

OSCAR F. BLACKWELDER

295. LIGHT BY LIFE

The atonement is never understood on the Christian level if it stops with any "moral influence" theory. God was in Christ reconciling the world to Himself, but not chiefly by giving us a light and a way. He gave us light by Life; He died to give us power for salvation. By accepting the fullness of the Love of God from Him who eternally is God, there came to be a union of God and man whereby a whole new stream of redemption was opened for man. This stream first came out of eternity; in history ever since the beginning of humanity the stream of grace had been making its hard and costly way against the stream of original sin. On Calvary the flood of grace broke through and became fully and openly available for man.

Nels F. S. Ferré

E. WITHOUT THE SHEDDING OF BLOOD

296. BLOOD OF THE LAMB

It is believed that in many churches to-day there is a reluctance to sing the blood of the Lamb; tastes have changed, we learn, and metaphors that once pleased please no longer. Yes, and theology changes. . . . But it stands that in the heart of the victorious church was written the story of the death of Christ, the central thing in all history, that in the blood of the Lamb was salvation from sin and victory over the world. It is worth remembering; and then we may ask why no great hymns have been written for a century; and as for those that have been written, they seem amenable to the stricture of St. Augustine on certain other literature—"what checked me was that the name of Christ was not there; and whatever lacked that name, however literary, however refined, however true, it did not wholly grip me" (*Confessions,* iii, 4, 8). No, the hymns of victory are the hymns of the Lamb, and "have His name written upon them" (xiv, 1).

T. R. Glover

297. DEADLY ARTIFICIALITY

Let those who are horrified by all this talk of blood beware lest they fall into the sentimentality by which no human soul is redeemed. In a day when whole cities may be filled with the blood of slaughtered peoples due to the pride and envy of men, it is not fitting for any sane person to be squeamish in speaking of the slaughtered Lamb of God. Indeed "it was real blood ran from His hands and the nail-holes." [1]... It is the deadliest kind of artificiality to speak in religion only of "sweetness and light" and to miss the cosmic symbolism in the cross of Christ, which is more than a symbol, for it bears in its own reality something of the divine reality it foreshadows. Is there or is there not at the heart of all things a Father-heart that suffers when his children suffer, that goes with them to their crosses, that bears their sins and forgives them because he made them to be worthy of eternal life? That is the question. The blood drops from the Cross of Christ declare that it is so, everlastingly so! The transformed redeemed of every age declare that it is so, presently so! The answering faith from your own heart this moment may know that it is so, graciously so!

LANCE WEBB

298. FUNCTION OF BLOOD

The function of blood is to nourish, to cleanse, to heal, and to keep in balance. Mankind is soul-sick with sin. We must all be healed. Apart from our coming "under the blood" of Christ there can be no healing. ... To be healed we must forsake our wretched self-seeking, our striving to be saved, and trust God who has Himself come, and who Himself comes, to save us by His blood. . . . Once healed, we must be cleansed over and over again. As the bloodstream flows into our lives and covers us wholly we are cleansed of our sins and made pure by the blood. The holiness of God has come basically with our being *healed* by the blood, but the holiness of God in us is ever in need of renewal. ... The blood also nourishes. We need to be fed on the Word of God. We need intellectual feeding, to be sure, but, more, we need the feeding of our spirits on the blood and body of Christ. Such feeding is no external act. It is entering within the universal community

[1] Carl Sandburg, "To a Contemporary Bunkshooter."

of Christ's love and sharing his life. . . . The blood also preserves the balance of the body. The process of interaction between metabolism and katabolism is dependent on the bloodstream. The blood carries the enzymes that keep harmony and balance in the life of the body. In the community of God is creative balance. God's love creates, maintains, and restores harmony to fellowship. Life is kept in order as we live within the bloodstream of God's love poured out for the world.

NELS F. S. FERRÉ

299. STRANGE POWER

Blood has a strange power. First, it cleanses the body of impurities, draws away the pus from injured tissues and restores them. Second, it even has the power of rebuilding tissues that have been destroyed. It builds not only skin and flesh, but, as in the case of the fingernail, it has the mysterious power of reproducing the structure and form as well. Third, the blood has the power of controlling the development of any part of the body, a power which reaches into the future.

Thus with the soul as well as the body. The blood not only brings redemption from sin but has the power to bring about development even to the point where a man feels himself to be a child of God. This conception of the mysterious power of blood was evidently that of Christ and his disciples. But the theological scholars of the nineteenth century were too rationalistic and rejected it. They did not see religion as related to life. They thought of the soul as an abstraction. But the soul does not exist apart from life.

The power of blood means the power of love! If blood can bring recovery to the sores of the body, love has the power to redeem the wounds of the personality. If blood has the power to restore broken-down tissues, love can make the wounded personality whole again, until it becomes a child of God. It is the teaching of the New Testament that the sacrificial love of Christ has this power to redeem and make restitution for all the past sins of humankind. Not that physical blood can redeem the sins of the soul; but to love other men enough to be willing to pour out your blood for them, this is the acme of spiritual love. Such love has the power to redeem and in this lies the hidden reason why Christ poured out his blood upon the cross.

TOYOHIKO KAGAWA

F. INTERPRETING THE CROSS

300. THE INTERPRETABLE CROSS

There are some who magnify the pathos of the Cross, and there are others who extol the heroism of it. It excites emotion in the breasts of those who contemplate it. There streams from the Cross an influence which produces a sense of awe and wonder. But it speaks as well. Its message is deeper and richer than that which can be conveyed through the presentation of the crucifix. It is charged with the capacity not only of quickening feelings, but also of awakening thoughts. In one of his noble frescoes, Giotto does justice to that fact. Faith is represented by him in the form of a figure holding a cross in one hand and a scroll in the other. The Cross is interpretable. The understanding of beholders is appealed to. It gives utterance to a word.

A. B. MACAULAY

301. GROWING GREATNESS

It is almost impossible to overemphasize the importance of the Cross. It is at the very heart of our religion. It presents an issue with which every Christian must deal. It is not a mere academic or theological question; it has to do with life itself. The more one studies it, the greater it grows.

In his old age, Tintoretto, the famous Venetian painter, asked to be taken once again to the seaside. He wanted to look upon the Adriatic another time. As his vision swept over the rolling waves, he exclaimed: "The sea always grows greater."

It is that way with the Cross. Its deeper meaning grows on us all the time.

G. RAY JORDAN

302. TRUTH ABOUT LIFE

The message of the Son of God who dies upon the cross, of a God who transcends history and is yet history, who condemns and judges sin and yet suffers with and for the sinner, this message is the truth about life. It cannot be stated without deceptions; but the truths which

141

seek to avoid the deceptions are immeasurably less profound. Compared to this Christ who died for men's sins upon the cross, Jesus, the good man who tells all men to be good, is more solidly historical. But he is the bearer of no more than a pale truism.

REINHOLD NIEBUHR

303. DIMENSIONS

From the earliest times the Cross has been the special sign of Christians. St. Paul tells us his great hope, his great business, what God had sent him into the world to do was this—to make people know the love of Christ; to look at Christ's Cross, and take in its breadth and length and depth and height.

And what is the *breadth* of Christ's Cross? My friends, it is as broad the whole world, for He died for the whole world; as it is written, "He is a propitiation not for our sins only, but for the sins of the whole world." And that is the *breadth* of Christ's Cross.

And what is the *length* of Christ's Cross? Long enough to last through all time. As long as there is a sinner to be saved; as long as there is ignorance, sorrow, pain, death, or anything else which is contrary to God and hurtful to man in the universe of God, so long will Christ's Cross last. And that is the *length* of the Cross of Christ.

And how *high* is Christ's Cross? As high as the highest heaven, and the throne of God and the bosom of the Father—that bosom out of which for ever proceed all created things. Ay, as high as the highest heaven; for, if you will receive it, when Christ hung upon the Cross heaven came down on earth, and earth ascended into heaven. And that is the *height* of the Cross of Christ.

And how *deep* is the Cross of Christ? This is a great mystery which people are afraid to look into, and darken it of their own will. But if the Cross of Christ be as high as heaven, then it must be as deep as hell, deep enough to reach the deepest sinner in the deepest pit to which he may fall, for Christ descended into hell, and preached to the spirits in prison. Let us hope, then, that is the *depth* of the Cross of Christ.

CHARLES KINGSLEY

304. CONFLICT AND CONQUEST

It is a very old story. You have all heard it hundreds of times. You know the details of it almost by heart; we preachers have told the story many, many times, and you might almost think that it would become hackneyed and trite and obvious. But it never does.

One reason for this is that it is a story of conflict, indeed the major conflict of life, the conflict between good and evil, the conflict between darkness and light, the conflict between life and death. And we all have our share of conflict. We have conflicts within ourselves, conflicts between the person we should like to be and the person we know we really are; we have conflicts between ourselves and our environment, our society and our world order and our civilization, and the demands they make upon us. We have family conflicts where will crosses will, just as the beams of the Cross crossed each other. So we have a particular interest in this story because of the nature of it. It is the story of a conflict, and conflicts concern us because we are so continually involved in them.

Then, of course, it is not only the story of a conflict but also the story of a conquest. It is the story of how the major conflict between good and evil was somehow not resolved, not eliminated, not escaped, not avoided, but redeemed, overcome, transcended. Thus the story gives us, in words we cannot define and cannot always understand or phrase specifically, the assurance that the conflicts in ourselves and the conflicts that exist between ourselves and the outside world can be conquered, that they need not end in frustration or defeat or despair, but there is a way to handle them. It has been done.

THEODORE PARKER FERRIS

G. BEARING THE CROSS

305. CONTINUAL DENIAL

The denying ourselves, and the taking up our cross, in the full extent of the expression, is not a thing of small concern: it is not expedient only, as are some of the circumstantials of religion; but it is absolutely, indispensably necessary, either to our becoming or continuing His disciples. It is absolutely necessary, in the very nature of the thing, to our coming after Him, and following Him; insomuch that, as far as we do not practice it, we are not His disciples. If we do not continually deny ourselves, we do not learn of Him, but of other masters. If we do not take up our cross daily, we do not come after Him, but after the world, or the prince of the world, or our own fleshly mind. If we are not walking in the way of the cross, we are not following Him; we are not treading in His steps; but going back from, or at least wide of, Him.

JOHN WESLEY

306. DO I FOLLOW?

No man has a right to be anything but afraid who follows Jesus. Where will it lead him? What about his family? What about his career? . . . We compromise, we make bargains with evil, we are not sure that what Jesus died for will work. We start out right, but when the shadow of the cross falls across our path, we find ways of framing a theology to suit our unregenerated natures. In a world of reality the cross will not work. Love is only for a perfectionist world. It all comes out of fear. We do not know to what foolish ends the cross will lead us. But the world is saved, not by the wisdom of men, but by the foolishness of the Gospel of Love. Whether the world will be saved by the cross depends upon what we decide. It is not "Do I understand?" but "Do I follow, whether I understand or not?" "Herein is love, not that we loved God, but that he loved us, and sent his Son." If God's love is generated in us we will be glad to choose the cross, and we will not hedge when we are discovered to be "one of them."

FREDERICK K. STAMM

307. "IF ANY MAN WOULD"

May I not drop the cross that grows so heavy,
Shorten the furrow-length that seems so long;
Must I pay tribute that the lilies levy,
Thrill to no music but a sparrow's song?

144

"Yea," speaks a voice all-gentle and all-knowing,
"Lighten your cross, look backward from your plow;
Gather the beauty your own hand is sowing,
Dance to the tune your heart is singing now.

"Choose! But recall in fortune or disaster—
Since 'tis yourself alone in judgment sits—
Who bears no cross follows another master
Who backward looks, another kingdom fits."

EDWIN McNEILL POTEAT

308. THE CROSS

How often will a man's own dream
Be made to serve as lateral beam,
With circumstance for upright, making
A cross his shoulders must be taking!

ADELAIDE LOVE

309. ASSUMING RESPONSIBILITIES

Taking up the cross is more than bearing manfully the burdens which
are the common lot of mortal men. To carry one's cross means assuming
responsibilities which could have been evaded. It requires fortitude to
endure the painful load plus love to forgive those who thus tax us.
Christ's cross-carriers are called to love their enemies, to bless those
that curse them, to do good to those that hate them, to pray for those
who despitefully use them and persecute them. Such demands seem at
first to be moral impossibles. And practical men say, surely God meant
us to use common sense. But as Arthur Clutton-Brock says: "Something greater, more beautiful, more passionate, than common sense
is needed, if we are to have common sense. . . . This is the paradox
of the Christian virtues. Common sense will not lead you to practice
them; you must see their beauty as something divine and worthy of
sacrifice, and then they will lead you to common sense."

RALPH W. SOCKMAN

H. ABOVE THE HILLS OF TIME

310. ABOVE THE HILLS OF TIME

Above the hills of time the Cross is gleaming,
    Fair as the sun when night has turned to day;
And from it love's pure light is richly streaming,
    To cleanse the heart and banish sin away.
To this dear Cross the eyes of men are turning
    Today as in the ages lost to sight;
And so for Thee, O Christ, men's hearts are yearning
    As shipwrecked seamen yearn for morning light.

The Cross, O Christ, Thy wondrous love revealing,
    Awakes our hearts as with the light of morn,
And pardon o'er our sinful spirits stealing
    Tells us that we, in Thee, have been reborn.
Like echoes to sweet temple bells replying,
    Our hearts, O Lord, make answer to Thy love;
And we will love Thee with a love undying,
    Till we are gathered to Thy home above.

THOMAS TIPLADY

311. CLOSED CASE

In the movie *The Life of Zola* there is a remarkable court scene. Zola was battling to reopen the Dreyfus affair, but his evidence was not admitted and his witnesses were not allowed to testify. Finally the judge declared that it was a closed case. As they were leaving the courtroom, Zola's lawyer pointed to a mural above the judge's head. It was a painting of the Crucifixion. The lawyer said, "That, too, was once regarded as 'a closed case.'"

That "closed case" of nineteen centuries ago was opened by the hand of the Eternal. God manifested his limitless power in the resurrection of his Son, who stepped forth from the shadows of the tomb in the power of an endless life. The disciples became new men.

Cowards were changed into heroes; pygmies became giants; broken reeds pillars of iron.

JOHN SUTHERLAND BONNELL

312. THE CROSS

When Christ went up the April roads
   The winds of April wept,
But through the woodway's early buds
   Triumphant murmur swept:
"On every height while time shall be
Shall shine the glory of a Tree."

CHARLES L. O'DONNELL

313. ATTRACTIVE POWER

Why should a stark Cross set against an Eastern sky offer such comfort and inward strength and hope and joy? What is this strange attractive power that draws living hearts and dying hearts to the uplifted Cross? You are not surprised at unhealthy-minded people going into rhapsody about the Cross. The delirious nonsense they talk is simply the outcome of false emotion, but when a distinguished soldier like Lord Roberts tells his soldiers that the death and sacrifice of Jesus is his sheet-anchor; when Sir James Mackenzie, the heart specialist, addresses a gathering of doctors and says to them, "Get a hold of what your Saviour's death should mean to you and your lives as medical men will become enlarged and enriched"; when Adolphe Monod, a Protestant professor at the Sorbonne in Paris, lies dying of cancer and cries in his agony, "The Cross! The Cross! O Christ, through pain I reach the mystery of Thy Cross! I am in Gethsemane at night, in Golgotha at morningtide, on Calvary at noon, but the remembrance of Thy Cross sustains me, oh, my Saviour!"; when Archbishop Temple writes to a friend, "My burden grows, but when it is heaviest I refresh my heart in my Redeemer's sacrifice"—when such men as these use such words as these—men notable for sanity, clear of brain, servants of truth and lovers of upright ways—surely it is wisdom on your part and mine to try to understand the the eternal charm and the magnetic power that has drawn, and still draws, the

147

heart of the world to a lonely man dying in pain upon a wooden Cross.

ALISTAIR MacLEAN

314. PERSISTENT LOVE

God alone can solve the dilemma of our sin, but His grace is thwarted unless we place our free hand in His proffered Hand. The initiatives, both in creation and in re-creation, are His; the needed responses are ours in His grace. We are not wax figures to be stamped in helplessness with the sign of the Cross: we are children who can, and should, assent to His gift, accepting it in answering love and in the endeavors of a renewed will. Calvary, on which Christ *gave* Himself to be crucified, does not coerce: it pleads in persistent love.

GEORGE A. BUTTRICK

315. I SEE MYSELF ARIGHT

I set the Cross with its physical agony alongside the desire of the body —my love of comfort, my continuous excuses for avoiding anything which may spoil that comfort. I set the Cross with all the naked and outcast poverty of it, the running out of a glorious life in premature death for the sake of a distant vision, beside my desire of the eye, my instant, childish itch to grasp any visible good thing, to enlarge and expand my present state, my fear to let the immediate delight go for a remoter and uncertain ideal, my subtle and permeating acquisitiveness. I set the Cross with its loneliness and shame alongside the empty vanities with which my beloved ego decks me out, even if it be only on the little stage my situation allows me. I remind myself that this is He whom I call Lord and for a moment, at least, I see myself as I am. I despise myself.

HERBERT H. FARMER

316. OH, THOU THAT FROM ETERNITY

Oh, Thou that from eternity
Upon Thy wounded heart hast borne

148

Each pang and cry of misery
   Wherewith our human hearts are torn,
Thy love upon the grievous cross
   Doth glow, the beacon-light of time,
Forever sharing pain and loss
   With every man in every clime.
How vast, how vast Thy sacrifice,
   As ages come and ages go,
Still waiting till it shall suffice
   To draw the last cold heart and slow!

HENRY N. DODGE

317. THOSE WHO PARTICIPATED

The church of Christ has the cross as the symbol of our redemption, and through the medium of a cross the church must continually call people to repentance. The establishment of the cross was possible because so many participated in it, and the justification of the cross is established when all classes and conditions and races and nations are saved through it. To establish the cross, the carpenters fashioned it, the metal workers forged the nails, the manual laborers dug the hole to receive it, the lawyers interpreted the law, the soldiers supplied the force, the priests gave it their blessing, and the stage was set. As men of all classes gathered around the cross, so men of all conditions can find their redemption in the cross.

H. E. D. ASHFORD

318. THE ONE AND THE MANY

Before the crucifixion Jesus Christ came as the Son of Man who joined Himself to the many in order to give Himself for them, the One representing the Many, but after the Pentecost and on the ground of the work on the Cross the Church was sent out as the Many to represent the One Son of Man, the Saviour Lord. Thus the relation of the One to the Many carries with it and begets the relation of the Many to the One. The One and the Many is the doctrine of Christ. The Many and the One is the doctrine of the Church, the body of Christ.

T. F. TORRENCE

319. PERPETUAL CHALLENGE

We are accustomed to think of the Cross in terms of forgiveness and reconciliation and new-found sources of moral power; and we have every right to do so, for behind all such thought there is the explicit teaching of the New Testament, and not only the explicit teaching of the New Testament but the radiant, transformed lives of men and women in every Christian generation. But the death of Jesus not only means that something amazing and wonderful has been done for us; it means that something demanding and exacting is expected of us. Christ on the Cross is a perpetual challenge to our world, and the head and front of the challenge is that we give up self-centered living. To avert our eyes from the Cross, to refuse to take up the challenge that confronts us there, is to proclaim ourselves devoid of two qualities for the want of which our civilization finds itself even now under sentence of decline and decay—the qualities of feeling and honour.

ROBERT J. McCRACKEN

I. OFFENSE OF THE CROSS

320. AMONG CHRIST'S CRUCIFIERS

The Cross is potentially effective for all the world; yet for some it is the organ of condemnation. Just as sacrifices in Israel that were not the organ of the soul's approach to God brought condemnation on men, so those for whom the sacrifice of Christ is not the organ of their approach to God stand under condemnation. "God sent not the Son into the world to condemn the world; but that the world through him might be saved. He that believeth on him is not condemned: but he that believeth not is condemned already." (John 3:18) Many who did not live in the days of Christ's flesh may find blessing and salvation through His Cross; but by the same token others who never saw Him may be guilty of the body and blood of Christ, or may crucify afresh the Son of God. While salvation is an external act, wrought by the power of God through the death of Christ, it is not wholly an external act, without relation to the spirit of men. Those who reject Christ, or who repudiate His way, share the iniquity of the crucifixion and stand before God in the company of Christ's crucifiers.

That is why the New Testament insists so much on faith. For faith is no mere intellectual belief, though it inevitably includes an intellectual element. But fundamentally it is not an integrated system of theology but the surrender of the person. When Jesus said to men, "Thy faith hath saved thee," He was not thinking in terms of a creed. He meant such a belief in Him that it involved the abandonment of the whole personality to Him, to be recreated by His touch and transformed into His own likeness. The woman who was a sinner and who bathed His feet with her tears heard Him say, "Thy faith hath saved thee; go in peace." (Luke 7:50) She did not return to her sin, for she went forth a changed woman. The self that loved the sin had died, and one now marked with the purity of Christ went forth to live in newness of life. This is what is meant by faith elsewhere in the New Testament. It is faith into Christ, faith that so indentifies a man with Him who was crucified that instead of being numbered with His crucifiers he becomes one with Christ, and the Cross becomes the organ of his submission of himself to God. Paul said "If we have become united with Him by the likeness of his death, we shall be also by the likeness of his resurrection; knowing this, that our old man was crucified with him, that the body of sin might be done away." (Rom. 6:5-6)

H. H. Rowley

321. ATTRACTION AND REPULSION

For the modern mind, as for the ancient, the attraction and the repulsion of Christianity are concentrated at the same point; the cross of Christ is man's only glory, or it is his final stumbling block.

James Denney

322. NO VITAL CONCERN

Of the many kinds of people whose footfall is rarely heard along the Way of the Cross, the largest group is the indifferent. To them the religion of Jesus Christ apparently is of no vital concern.

Some are apt to be among the nicest people we know. They are pleasant, kindly, hard-working, take a share in the community, prosper and give every evidence of pursuing well-rounded lives. They would be shocked if told that they live lop-sided. They wouldn't dream of being combative or argumentative or vicious about religion. They wouldn't dream of crucifying Christ. They simply ignore Him.

RICHARDSON WRIGHT

323. CHRIST IS CRUCIFIED ANEW

Not only once, and long ago,
There on Golgotha's rugged side,
Has Christ, the Lord, been crucified
Because He loved a lost world so.
But hourly souls, sin-satisfied,
Mock His great love, flout His commands.
And I drive nails deep in His hands,
You thrust the spear within His side.

JOHN RICHARD MORELAND

324. MOMENTARY REVERENCE

That is a disturbing story which Francis Turner Palgrave, the compiler of *The Golden Treasury,* tells in his diary, describing the behavior of the mob that invaded the Palace of the Tuileries during the French Revolution. The mob had gone through several rooms. They were intent upon looting and destroying what they saw. It was a violent, shrieking crowd of enraged people. They burst open a closed door, to find themselves suddenly in the palace chapel. There above the altar was an appropriate painting. It was of Christ being crucified. A hush fell upon this furious crowd of enraged men. Somebody cried out, "Hats off!" Every head was bowed. Then before one realized what was occurring, the crowd knelt. Reverence and awe laid hold upon them.

Then in the silence of that holy reverence, somebody went forward and took down the picture from the altar. It was placed in a neighboring church. But when the picture was removed, the tide of destruction rolled on.

G. RAY JORDAN

VIII. Day of Triumph

A. EASTER

325. DAY OF GOOD TIDINGS

This is a day when perplexities cannot stay, fears cannot tarry with us, our heads cannot long hang down; the news of it is so full of gladness, of comfort, and of joy. At the rising of this day's sun of righteousness, our perplexities pass away as the clouds before the sun; our tears melt as the dew before it; and we turn up our heads like flowers to the sunbeams. It is a day the fullest of all good things—as the seal and assurance of all the good news we heard before it. The angels fly everywhere about today, even into the grave, with comfortable messages. "Why weepest thou?" says one; "Fear not," says another; "Why seek" you "among the dead?" says a third. What do you at the grave?—"He is risen," says the whole choir; he whose rising is all your risings, who is your Saviour now complete, and the lifter up of all your heads; and go but into Galilee and you shall see him.

MARK FRANK

326. HIS DAY, NOT OURS

Easter Day is like the wedding-day of an intimate friend: our impulse as Christians is to forget ourselves, and to think only of the great Object of our sympathies. On Good Friday we were occupied with ourselves; with our sins, our sorrows, our resolutions. If we entered into the spirit of that day at all, we spread these out, as well as we could, before the dying eyes of the Redeemer of the world; we asked Him, of His boundless pity, to pardon and to bless us. To-day is His day, as it seems, not ours. It is His day of triumph; His day of re-asserted rights and recovered glory; and our business is simply to forget ourselves; to intrude with nothing of our own upon hours which are of right consecrated to Him; to think of Him alone; to enter with simple, hearty, disinterested joy upon the duties of congratulation and worship which befit the yearly anniversary of His great victory.

H. P. LIDDON

327. RIGHT SIDE OF EASTER

This broken, warring world is living on the wrong side of Easter Day. That is the basic fact, and the source of all our troubles. We are back where the disciples were, between Good Friday and the Resurrection. Like them, we are groping in the dark. We are on the wrong side of Easter. We are standing helpless before the towering mystery of evil's tragic dominion, feeling our hopeless inadequacy in the face of the grim facts of sin and chaos and man's ruthless inhumanity to man. We are still fighting the spectres of the night, still searching pathetically for some man-made, humanistic solution to our problems, struggling in the morass of fear and impotence and confusion. And the supreme need of the world at this moment is to start living on the other side—the right side—of Easter. It is to know that in the Resurrection of Jesus God Himself has spoken, and God's empire of righteousness and peace and joy and liberty has been brought decisively to light.

JAMES S. STEWART

328. EASTER LIGHT

Because upon the first
    glad Easter day,
The stone that sealed His tomb
    was rolled away,
So, through the deepening shadows
    of death's night,
Men see an open door . . .
    beyond it, light.

IDA NORTON MUNSON

329. YET MORE THAN ALL

The hearts of men are candles—
(Lord, touch the wick with fire.)
The hearts of men are candles
To burn with swift desire.

Oh, Christ, how strange the yearning—
(More strange than all beside!)
The hearts of men are burning—
A light for Easter-tide.

ELEANOR SLATER

330. STRENGTH FOR LIFE

Easter day says to us, if you labour to create good company in this
life, by trying to make other people round you good, you shall enjoy
for ever in the next world the good company which you have helped to
make. If you labour to make yourself good in this life, you shall enjoy
the fruit of your labour in the next life by being good, and, therefore,
blessed for ever. Easter day says, your labour is not vanity and vexa-
tion of spirit. It is solid work, which shall receive solid pay from God
hereafter. Easter day is a pledge—I may say a sacrament—from God
to us, that He will righteously reward all righteous work; and that,
therefore, it is worth any man's while to labour, to suffer, if need be
even to die, in trying to be good, noble, useful, self-sacrificing, as Christ
toiled and suffered and died and sacrificed Himself to do good. For
then he will share Christ's reward, as he has shared Christ's labour,
and be rewarded as Christ was, by resurrection to eternal life. And
so Easter day should give us strength to live like men—the only truly
manly, truly human life; the life of being good and doing good.

CHARLES KINGSLEY

331. WE NEED NOT DESPAIR

Let us not make Easter merely an opportunity to discuss the values
of eternal life. That has its worth, and certainly Jesus came that
we might reach up to such a thought and lay hold upon its deepest

truth. But let us at this time of darkness remember that Easter also means the possibility of joy in the midst of pain, of light in the midst of darkness, of hope in the midst of despair. Easter is the guarantee of God that joy can triumph in the affairs of men. Jesus rose from his death couch not only to seal life for men, but also to give them that deathless happiness that comes to those who have looked upon the face of God. There are many things in the future that seem hopeless; but so long as we have the knowledge of this marvelous fact of Easter we will not despair, but will continue well assured that though the night be heavy round about us, joy cometh with the morning. "All shall yet be well," is the promise of Easter.

WILLIAM E. PHIFER, JR.

332. EASTER EMPHASIS

In recent years there has been a decided change in the emphasis given to Easter from the average pulpit. Not many years ago many ministers felt that it was their inescapable duty to offer some positive proof by which the authenticity of our Lord's resurrection might be substantiated. Then there followed a time when most ministers dwelt especially upon the certainty of our own resurrection and the comfort it gives us to know that death is not the end of our experience, but the beginning of a far more meaningful and rewarding one. Now, however, we appear to be in an era in which a third emphasis is being made—an emphasis which reminds us that, for the Christian, the resurrection must be a present experience as well as a thing to be anticipated in the future.

EDWARD HUGHES PRUDEN

333. CHURCH OF THE RESURRECTION

Apart from Easter, all would remain shrouded in darkness. Without Easter the Jews were right when they mocked Him for His claim to be the Son of God: a criminal who had been hanged!—Son of God! Easter alone brings out the fact that in this "form of a servant" the King was really concealed.

Therefore the message of Easter is the Christian message, and the Christian Church is the Church of the Resurrection. This is true from the historical point of view: it was not until Easter had taken place that the Church was formed. On Good Friday there was no Church; all the disciples of the Lord were scattered as sheep that have no shepherd. It was the fact of Easter which drew them together. It was this fact alone which made Peter truly understand the truth that had previously simply shot through his mind like a flash of lightning: "Verily Thou art the Son of the Living God." Easter alone made a full belief in Christ possible. If the "movement" were to be real, its meaning could only be fulfilled at the point where it was perfected. A speculative belief in Easter? What nonsense! As a woman can only sew properly with a knotted thread—for otherwise her work would be in vain—so if Christ be not risen, really risen from the dead, and has actually been "seen" as the Risen Lord, all Christian faith is vain. Everything else is pure fallacy. Positively as well as historically—this coincidence is necessary—Easter is the foundation stone of the Christian faith and of the Christian Church.

EMIL BRUNNER

334. EITHER . . . OR

Has the Easter message we have so often heard really made much difference in our living? There is an inevitable drift of things in life. We are fluid, not static. Either life as it progresses becomes very pregnant with meaningful things, or by the same token it becomes more and more empty and meaningless. Life can be poor, or it can be rich. These tendencies are universal. The steady rhythmic beats of time produce within us either life or death. Life and death eternal are present, not post mortem, possessions. Immortality may be good or it may be bad, depending upon whether we choose to be with God or away from God. Eternal death is always away from God. Either we are immortally with God or we are immortally away from God. But who would honestly care for an existence after death if it must be apart from God? Eternal life begins here and now. The disciples who walked with Jesus came to possess it, and the faithful ones of every age have learned to know its gracious meaning, its precious value. It was the Savior who by His resurrection "brought life and immortality to light."

OLIN S. REIGSTAD

335. YOU CANNOT GET RID OF EASTER

Even if we fail to choose God's Easter beckoning in glad response to His grace, we cannot get rid of Easter. Soon or late we must come to terms with the Resurrection. The Mosque of St. Sophia in Istanbul was originally a Christian church, though the Christian symbols and inscriptions have been overlaid. A visitor noticed, as he stood under the great dome, that a picture of the ascendant Christ, his arms outstretched in blessing, was showing through the covering paint; and the visitor exclaimed, almost despite himself, "He is coming back. You cannot blot him out"! If you wish to prophesy, with some chance of success, in a world which seems to falsify all man's guesses, prophesy that Christ will come back when the cruel simplification of Communism, the greedy self-entanglements of capitalism, and the dull average of socialism have all been forgotten. Even if men fail the Easter beckoning, God in the present Spirit of Jesus will not fail us.

GEORGE A. BUTTRICK

336. POST-EASTER PROGRAM

One of the saddest things about our modern observance of Easter is our neglect of Jesus' great post-Easter program. We are all perfectly willingly to rejoice with Him on Easter day and to share in His triumph over death and the grave. What a splendid thrill sweeps over the soul when the choir sings and when, amid the ecstasy of beauty, joy, and hope, we feel that we, too, know that our Redeemer liveth and that, though we perish, yet shall we live and be like Him and never die. All that on Easter, all that with a fervor that is fine and deep, and then on the Sunday following Easter, what do we find? A tired and scanty congregation of elderly folks, possibly? The same old wearisome problems, the same old indifference and coldness, the same lack of spirit, the same unwillingness to dare and to do and to die? To be sure, I am not charging any particular congregation with all this. At the same time, will you not agree with me that often this spirit is found in greater or lesser degree and that, wherever it manifests itself in close proximity to such a day and season as Easter, it is particularly unworthy and unwarranted?

GERHARD E. LENSKI

159

337. AFTER EASTER

On Easter day my heart is lifted high
With gladsome praises to the Lord of life.
The hallelujahs ring: the heavens are rife
With song and story. He who could defy
The powers of death has risen again—is nigh
To say, "Fear not ... Men, put away your strife,
I am the resurrection and the life."
All earth seems joyous, and we need not die!

The vision fades; the Easter joy is past;
Again in dull drab paths our lot is cast.
The heavens no longer sing. The war clouds lower.
O Lord, where art Thou in Thy risen power?
The calm voice speaks—it answers all I ask,
"I am beside you in the daily task."

GEORGIA HARKNESS

B. CROSS AND CROWN

338. CALVARY AND EASTER

A song of sunshine through the rain,
  Of Spring across the snow;
A balm to heal the hurts of pain,
  A peace surpassing woe.
Lift up your heads, ye sorrowing ones,
  And be ye glad of heart,
For Calvary and Easter Day,
Earth's saddest day and gladdest day,
  Were just three days apart!

SUSAN COOLIDGE

339. THIS SIDE OF CALVARY

We live on this side of Calvary. Had we lived on the other side of it, could we by any possible chance have expected to see the glory of the

Resurrection, the transformation in the lives and outlook of the disciples, and the on-moving triumph of the great cause of Christ? He wrote no books; he formed no great organization; his followers were, for the most part, "ignorant and unlearned men and women." He exercised his ministry among a subject people of no particular political importance. Falling foul of the authorities, he was condemned to a shameful death, and his followers were dispersed in terror lest a similar fate befall them. Today the faith of Jesus is stronger than it has ever been. Millions throughout the centuries have loved him and today thousands upon thousands are prepared to spend their lives in his service. To ponder the story of the Cross and its amazing sequel is to be established in a faith that fosters great expectations and boundless hopes.

JOHN SHORT

340. GOOD FRIDAY: EASTER SUNDAY

Good Friday in my heart! Fear and affright!
My thoughts are the Disciples when they fled,
My words the words that priest and soldier said,
My deed the spear to desecrate the dead.
And day, Thy death therein, is changed to night.

Then Easter in my heart sends up the sun.
My thoughts are Mary, when she turned to see.
My words are Peter, answering, "Lov'st thou Me?"
My deeds are all Thine own drawn close to Thee,
And night and day, since Thou dost rise, are one.

MARY ELIZABETH COLERIDGE

341. KEEP ON WATCHING

The most vivid portrayal of the trial, crucifixion, and resurrection of Christ that I have ever seen was on television one Sunday afternoon. Had I known what was coming, I think I would have turned to something else and not have let our two little children (aged four and

161

six) see it, but after it started we decided to let them see it all the way through.

They see all the fighting, shooting, and killing in the Wild West pictures, but that doesn't bother them; they know it isn't real. But this was Jesus! Since they were old enough to learn, they had been taught that Jesus was good and kind and that He loved everybody. They sing "Jesus loves me, this I know," and they have come to love Him.

They saw men whipping Him and it broke their hearts. When He was nailed to the cross, they cried. They had heard about the cross, but it had never been so real to them before. They could hardly bear it. Then He was buried, and I have never seen two more confused and unhappy children.

I told them to keep on watching and see what happened. Then Easter morning came. There were the women on the way to the tomb, feeling just as our own little children felt. But the resurrection came. He rose out of the grave and walked in the garden.

And what a marvelous relief and joy showed on the faces of those two little children. That little four-year-old girl gleefully said, "Jesus is all right. He has 'arised.'" The fact that everything came out so well in the end was all they needed to know.

CHARLES L. ALLEN

342. INCARNATE LOVE ARISES

The Cross without the Resurrection might be a bitter irony. Granted Christ is our Sun, His light is still darkness if the Sun has forever set. If Jesus just died, and if that is the end of Him, the sting of death is not drawn. The sin might then be in God, for the God who could extinguish such a life would hardly be Godlike. The work of God would be indicated, the universe would be impeached; for it would be careful of its dust and careless of its virtue—like some vandal who destroys a great canvas but treasures its threads. In any event, if Jesus is blown out like a match, our redemption is blown out like a match. There is no hope in a pro-tem Jesus: He must be resurrection and eternal life. When the revolutionists in France proposed a new "philosophical" religion, Talleyrand, it is reported, advised them, "The matter is simple: you have only to get yourself crucified, and then at your own time rise from the dead, and you will have no trouble."

Because he was Talleyrand, his tests were still shallow. It is *not* enough to be crucified and rise. Many men have been crucified who, if they had risen, would have been a returning threat rather than salvation. But Talleyrand was right about the rising from the dead. He should have said, "You have only to incarnate Holy Love, get yourself crucified, and rise from the dead."

GEORGE A. BUTTRICK

343. CLUE TO THE LIFE

The Gospel writers have been criticized for spending so much time telling the story of Jesus' death instead of telling us more about his life. The thing which these critics do not see is that the death and life of Jesus are all of a piece. If his life sheds light on his death, then his death also sheds light on his life. In other words, the writers had the feeling that when they came to an understanding of the Crucifixion and the Resurrection, they had the essential clue to the Life. The sharp division which we moderns tend to make between a man's life and his death is meaningless and unreal to these Christian writers. They felt that the way a man dies gives the light we need in satisfactorily understanding his life.

GERALD KENNEDY

344. THE STONE ROLLED AWAY

Grave could not hold the Lord Christ then,
Nor the conspiracy of men.
Mausoleums of our books
Where the seeking spirit looks
Are inadequate to bind
His illimitable mind.

Read the Truth in each new age
Written on some heart's bright page.
Life translating Life may give
Doubt a sure affirmative.

ELINOR LENNEN

345. TRAGEDY AND TRIUMPH

By the Cross and the Resurrection the local Christ becomes the universal Christ, the Christ of a swiftly-transacted earthly ministry becomes the Christ for the world's entire after-time, let that stretch far forward as it may. There is of course more than this to be said of both His death and His rising; but this is the idea within which all else is enclosed and out of which consequently all else springs. And let it be emphasized at once, and borne in memory throughout, that Cross and Resurrection must be taken *together* if the significance of either is to be grasped. To isolate the Cross from the subsequent reversal of its tragedy, and to treat the first as if that alone constituted the supreme event in which Christ became the world's Redeemer, while looking upon the second as being not much more than a miracle whereby Christ's title and competence (if the poor word may pass) to have performed the redemptive work are proved, is to separate two halves of one double-sided entity and by the severance to blur the contour and lose the true vision of the whole. Yet this is in effect the line on which much discussion of the theme proceeds. It is like dividing a jewel in two. Each segment of it may indeed remain wonderful enough in itself, but the more excellent glory of the perfect gem is not thus yielded to one's gazing eyes. Cross and Resurrection taken *together* make the life-dynamic in Christ available for all the ages and for all the world. They are not so much two successive events as two constituent elements in one transcendent event. Christ, because He died *and* because He rose again, lives here and everywhere—will be living everywhere while the ages run—and will therefore be everywhere and always what He was when He lived on earth, the Christ who brings the veritable life of God to the human plane and communicates it ceaselessly to all the generations of mankind. Through the tragedy and the triumph, taken *together,* He stands out as the Lord of life, as Jesus Christ the same yesterday and to-day and for ever.

Henry W. Clark

346. O RISEN CHRIST

O Risen Christ, who know'st my heart
That longs to play its greatest part,

Shuns Friday's crowd that crucified,
To take its stand thy Cross beside,
Save me from the sin, I pray,
Of living in Easter Saturday
And let each day for me be full
Of Easter Sunday's miracle

MORRIS MARTIN

C. THESE WERE HIS WITNESSES

347. HE WILL RESPOND

Mary standing without weeping is a concrete representative of a not
uncommon state of mind. She stands wondering why she was ever so
foolish, so heartless, as to leave the tomb at all. It is thus that those
who have been careless about maintaining communion with Christ
reproach themselves when they find He is gone. The ordinances, the
prayers, the quiet hours of contemplation that once were filled with
Him are now like the linen clothes and the napkin, empty, cold, pale
forms of His presence that make His absence all the more painful. And
yet this self-reproach is itself a seeking to which He will respond. To
mourn His absence is to desire and to invite His presence, and to
invite His presence is to secure it.

MARCUS DODS

348. WE RECOGNIZE MARY

Mary Magdalene, weeping before the empty tomb of Jesus, reappears
in each generation of Christians; it is not hard, at least for some of
us, to recognize her among ourselves. She is the type of those who have
a genuine love of religion, but who from whatever cause, and in
various ways, are for a time, at any rate, disappointed. And religious
disappointment is difficult to bear, in proportion to the genuineness
and sincerity of a man's character: because it is felt that much is im-
perilled, while such disappointment lasts. For religion invites a larger
stake—a bolder investment of thought and feeling and purpose than
any other subject, corresponding to its transcendent importance. And

when those who have given up all else that they may win this, think that they have missed what they hoped to have; when those who like the merchant in the parable have sold their all to buy the pearl of great price, and suppose, though it be without reason, and only for a short while, that they have bought a flint after all; the recoil of baffled hope is even terrible.

H. P. LIDDON

349. SLOW OF HEART

No reasonable criticism can explain away the picture we are given of the Apostles' "hardened" state of mind in face of the idea of the Cross before the Crucifixion, and the mental gloom into which the event plunged them—so that the first reports of the resurrection "seemed to them but idle tales"; nor can any reasonable criticism lead us to doubt the picture we are given of them a few weeks later—confident, radiant men, ready to face what would have seemed to be the impossible task of converting a hostile world to the new Gospel—ready for anything, including death itself. Such they are, because they feel their feet resting on an unshakable rock of experience, the experience of Christ risen and alive, which had given a wholly new colour to their minds and orientation to their lives. Such a complete mental change in this whole body of unimaginative men—really "slow of heart"— must have had some very solid cause. They would not have been forced round so sharp a corner to such a new outlook on life except by some very definite force. And there is not any reasonable ground for doubting that they would have ascribed their conversion to the fact that they had repeatedly seen their Lord.

CHARLES GORE

350. DIVINE ENTHUSIASM

When the Master stood before Thomas and his friends in that little upper room so long ago, and held out his wounded hands to them, it was a call to war. A divine enthusiasm was kindled in their souls, an enthusiasm for him, a willingness to dare anything and everything in the cause for which he had suffered and died. The appearance of

Jesus on the inner side of those closed doors meant that before long they were flung wide open, that a dauntless band of warriors might go forth to do battle in his invincible name. The very things they had been afraid of before he came, they were afraid of no longer— neither shame, nor scorn, nor loss of friends and worldly goods, nor bonds and stripes, nor poverty and starvation, nor death itself in whatsoever guise it might come.

R. J. CAMPBELL

351. THE NEW TESTAMENT APPEARANCES

These are the appearances referred to in the New Testament as having taken place between Easter morning and the Day of Ascension itself or the appearance to Paul. They are as follows: (1) appearance to Mary Magdalene (Mark 16:9-11; John 20:11-18); (2) appearance to the company of women (Matt. 28:9, 10); (3) appearance to Peter (Luke 24:34; 1 Cor. 15:5); (4) appearance to the two disciples on the road to Emmaus (Mark 16:12-13; Luke 24:13-35); (5) appearance to the ten apostles in Jerusalem, Thomas being absent (Luke 24:36-43; John 20:19-23; since Mark speaks of eleven disciples, I would not include his reference here but in the sixth appearance); (6) appearance again to the apostles eight days later, Thomas being present (John 20:24-29 and possibly Mark 16:14); (7) appearance on the Lake of Galilee to the seven apostles (John 21); (8) appearance to the five hundred in Galilee (Matt. 28:16-20; 1 Cor. 15:6); (9) appearance to James (1 Cor. 15:7).

This of course is not necessarily the order in which the appearances occurred. There could have been more than these. Indeed, from interpretation of Matt. 28:16 and 1 Cor. 15:6 I am inclined to believe Jesus met first with the eleven in Galilee, later with the five hundred. The appearance at the Ascension is given in Luke 24:50-51; Acts 1:6-9.

WILLIAM R. CANNON

352. TWO ENDS IN VIEW

In this first interview of our risen Lord with His disciples as a body (John 20:21-23), there seem to be two ends which He has in view.

The one is to assure them of the reality of the resurrection; the other is to open up its bearings and consequences. Hence, for the first purpose, He met them with the old salutation of peace upon His lips, and then showed them His hands and His side, that He might convince them of the truth of His rising and of His identity, not only in body, but also in mind. All this had the desired effect, and the disciples "were glad when they saw the Lord." But beyond this was the second and kindred end of our Lord's words and acts in this earliest meeting, since it was very important to cast light upon the meaning of the resurrection which had been accomplished, and to show all that had been gained for the Church, as well as for the Saviour Himself in that great victory. . . . We are here taught that Christ's resurrection is the pledge of peace to His people. . . . Christ's resurrection is the authorisation of the gospel ministry. . . . Christ's resurrection is the unsealing of spiritual influence. . . . The resurrection of Christ is the investiture of His Church with absolving and condemning power.

JOHN CAIRNS

353. MORE THAN AN APPEARANCE

There is no such thing in the New Testament as an appearance of the Risen Saviour in which He merely appears. He is always represented as entering into relation to those who see Him in other ways than by a flash upon the inner or outer eye: He establishes other communications between Himself and His own than that which can be characterised in this way. It may be that a tendency to materialise the supernatural has affected the evangelical narrative here or there—that Luke, for instance, who makes the Holy Spirit descend upon Jesus in bodily form as a dove went involuntarily beyond the apostolic tradition in making the Risen One speak of His flesh and bones, and eat a bit of roast fish before the disciples, to convince them that He was no mere ghost; it may be so, though the mode of Christ's being, in the days before His final withdrawal, is so entirely beyond our comprehension, that it is rash to be too peremptory about it; but even if it were so, it would not affect the representation as a whole which the gospels give of the Resurrection, and of the relation of the Risen One to His disciples. It would not affect the fact, that He not only appeared to them, but spoke to them. It would not affect the fact, that He not only appeared to them, but taught them, and in particular gave them a commission in which the meaning of His own life and work, and their calling as connected with it, are finally declared.

JAMES DENNEY

354. RESURRECTION GLORY

Last of all He was seen of me also.
1 CORINTHIANS 15:8.

And by that vision Saul of Tarsus was transformed. And so, by the ministry of a risen Lord we have received the gift of a transfigured Paul. The resurrection glory fell upon him, and he was glorified. In that superlative light he discovered his sin, his error, his need, but he also found the dynamic of the immortal hope.

"Seen of me also!" Can I, too, calmly and confidently claim the experience? Or am I altogether depending upon another man's sight, and are my own eyes unillumined? In these realms the witness of "hear-says" counts for nothing; he only speaks with arresting power who has "seen for himself."

JOHN HENRY JOWETT

355. KNOWN IN FELLOWSHIP

Though individuals had their own experiences of the risen Christ, it was in fellowship with one another that they knew him most fully. Not only faith and hope and courage, but the love that he lived and taught, surged up in their lives and transformed them into "his body." The Church which thus came to birth exists because of the Resurrection. As through the centuries it has grown from a handful of men and women to uncounted millions, its Scriptures, its sacred day, its Church Year, its sacraments, its creeds, its fellowship, and its outreaching service all continue to witness to "his mighty resurrection." Wherever the Church has fully appropriated the resurrection faith, it has experienced "the immeasurable greatness of his power in us who believe, according

169

to the working of his great might which he accomplished in Christ when he raised him from the dead." (Eph. 1:19 f.).

WALLACE EUGENE ROLLINS
MARION BENEDICT ROLLINS

D. MANY INFALLIBLE PROOFS

356. DIRECT EVIDENCE

What is the more direct evidence which the historian must investigate: (a) It is important, first, to notice that the Resurrection was not expected. The available evidence suggests that neither the Scriptures nor the words of Jesus had led the disciples to a conviction that He would rise again. If the predictions by Jesus of His Passion went home to the disciples, the predictions of the Resurrection (if indeed He made such predictions explicitly) caused no clear expectation. . . .

(b) Next, there is the evidence provided by the existence of the Church in spite of the catastrophe of Good Friday. What happened so to change the disciples from survivors of a cause that was broken and crushed into men who could bid the nation to repent and be baptized into the name of Christ, and could proclaim even the Crucifixion itself to be a Gospel? This is a question that the historian cannot avoid. . . .

(c) There is the evidence that the disciples became subject to the impact of Jesus Christ moulding their minds and hearts. This is evidence from religious experience, and it is beset by the difficulties and limitations which belong to such evidence. But evidence it is. . . . The testimony cannot easily be dismissed . . . and it is related not to a narrow field of religion or emotion but to the whole of life wherein thinking, feeling and action were made creative under the new and unexpected impulse. . . .

(d) There is the evidence that Jesus appeared to the disciples. We find this evidence in Paul's statements about himself, in the tradition that Paul received concerning other Apostles, and in the narratives in the Gospels. . . .

(e) There is, lastly, the evidence that the women found the tomb empty upon the third day after the Crucifixion and reported the news to the Apostles. This evidence is set forth in the Gospels. Mark describes the visit of the women; John follows a separate tradition of a visit by Mary Magdalene alone. According to John—and some mss. of Luke—Apostles came to the tomb to verify the news for themselves.

A. MICHAEL RAMSEY

357. INDUBITABLE CERTAINTY

Of the fact of the Resurrection, Paul had not a shadow of a doubt. It was one of his indubitable certainties. He himself had had a revelation of the Lord, which had altered the whole tenor of his life. He had known and conversed with those who saw Him in the days that followed upon Easter morning. Whatever might be doubtful to his intellect, or might remain a matter of conjecture, his life, both of experience and thought, was based upon the fact that Christ was risen. But the power of a fact is to be distinguished from the fact itself. The power is the influence it exercises in its various relationships to life. And so the power of the Resurrection is not the power that raised Christ from the dead, but the increasing pressure upon life of the stupendous fact that Christ is risen. To penetrate more fully into this, to grasp it in its infinite significance, that was the ambition of St. Paul as he made his lonely way among the mysteries. Like some bright star the fact was always shining. It was unalterable and unsetting. His passion was to know the power of the fact.

GEORGE H. MORRISON

358. REALITY OF THE RESURRECTION

If we are faithful to the evidence, we must start from the fact of the empty tomb. The theory that the body of Jesus was stolen or hidden is frankly incredible. Had the Romans or the Jews removed it secretly, it would have been easy to refute the Christians' claim by producing it. We may be sure that they did not, because they could not. Equally incredible, as even a Jew like Klausner admits, is the suggestion that the disciples hid his body and then went forth to declare that Jesus had risen from the dead. If then we accept the empty tomb, one of two explanations is open to us. Either we say that Jesus was resuscitated from the grave in his former body—in which case we must face the problem of what eventually happened to it after "the forty days," or we may agree with a long line of Christians from St. Paul to Bishop Westcott, that the physical body of our Lord was transformed in the grave into a spiritual body, a body no longer subject to the ordinary limitations of space and time. It is worth noticing here how evangelists like St. Luke and St. John, despite all differences, agree about the nature of the Lord's risen body. On the one hand, what they tell us suggests something quite un-earthly, since Jesus can come and go through closed doors and appear and disappear at will. On the other hand, the risen body has earthly features, since Jesus is said to have eaten and to have allowed himself to be touched. This combination of unearthly and earthly features, the evangelists testify, characterized the reality of the Resurrection. This suggests that, in trying to fathom the mystery of the first Easter Day, we should think of something essentially otherworldly—a piece of heavenly reality—invading this world of time and sense and manifesting itself to those with "eyes of faith." We are concerned with an unmistakably divine event which yet occurred in this world of ours, on an April day in A.D. 30 while Pontius Pilate was Roman governor in Judea.

ARCHIBALD M. HUNTER

359. THE LIVING CHURCH

The proof of the Resurrection is the living Church of Jesus Christ. The life of the Church proves the life of the Saviour. When Jesus Christ died, His disciples, as might be expected, were plunged in profound despair. When the Shepherd was smitten, the flock was scattered abroad. But no long time had passed before a great revolution took place. They were at first in despair in spite of all that He had said. His enemies were quicker to discern the meaning of His prophecies than His disciples, and their fears were stronger than His disciples' hopes. No collapse could be imagined more complete than that which took place at the entombment of the Saviour; but in a little time all was changed. The men who before had been cowards, slow of heart to believe, were completely transformed. They became brave and strong, and full of the most resolved faith. It was not that their outward circumstances had changed. They were sheep in the midst of wolves, and the beginning of their conflict with the world might have been expected to disappoint rather than encourage them;

but instead of that, they have a new faith in the power of Jesus Christ—a faith which transforms them and makes them men. What explains this: Something must have happened in the interval to account for so marvellous a transformation. Nothing can explain it, save the Resurrection of Jesus Christ. That Resurrection breathed into them new faith, and hope, and strength, by virtue of which they faced fearlessly the most formidable odds, and most determined enemies. That is the explanation of Paul. It has never been denied, even by the extremest scepticism, that the First Epistle to the Corinthians was written within thirty-five years after the death of Christ. In that Epistle the whole gospel is built on the risen Christ. Jesus had broken the fetters of the tomb—the Lord had risen indeed; and in the strength of that risen Lord His disciples were henceforth to fight.

WILLIAM ROBERTSON NICOLL

E. MEANINGS OF HIS RESURRECTION

360. NEW PERSPECTIVE

We who have grown up, familiar all our lives with the accepted fact of the Resurrection and with at least some of its implications, cannot imagine what it must have meant to the earliest followers of Christ. To feel that hated Rome, with all her terrifying display of power, could not do anything more to the beloved and risen Saviour, and to feel *that,* after feeling on the night of the Crucifixion that all was over like a beautiful dream that ends in a shattering awakening—this, I say, we cannot comprehend. But on top of that, to feel convinced, as they did, that no shadowy Hades, such as the rabbis had taught—and indeed such as the Old Testament still pictures—was theirs, but joyous and uninterrupted reunion with Christ and with their own loved ones—this must have been wonder upon wonder. More wonderful even than this, in my opinion, was the conviction that the values he had taught and exemplified were established. The power of evil was shattered. It could not debase them. Rome, after all, was a passing evil. Permanence belonged to the kingdom of love and truth and faith. Immortality came to *light* through the gospel. Where all had been dark, vague, shadowy, and unreal, the Resurrection put this earth-life in a completely new perspective. It gave meaning and purpose to events which otherwise seemed to point to an unjust or callous or blundering God.

LESLIE D. WEATHERHEAD

361. JESUS IS LORD

Early Christians did not go out into the world preaching an ethical code, or a system of philosophy, or a utopian gospel of social improvement. Those who think that the essence of Christianity in the New Testament period was the Sermon on the Mount, or the doctrine of the "Fatherhood of God and the brotherhood of man," have the evidence of critical, historical scholarship against them. The Church was established on the Resurrection faith, summed up in the creedal affirmation: Jesus is Lord. This is not to deny the importance of the Fatherhood of God or the Sermon on the Mount. We are merely demanding that these matters be placed within their proper context of faith if one is to do justice to the New Testament. Christianity is not just the belief in one God; Christians worship the God who raised Christ from the dead (see Romans 4:24; I Peter 1:21; and so on). Christianity is not just a noble ethic; ethical motivation arises from the fact that men are "raised together with Christ" in order that they may "walk in newness of life" (Col. 3:1; Rom. 6:4). Christianity is the religion of the Resurrection. Herein lies its distinctiveness and power.

BERNHARD W. ANDERSON

362. RESURRECTION EXPERIENCE

Dr. Ernest F. Scott says the disciples were not primarily men of ideas; they were men of action. They did not have a concept of immortality, and then think up a resurrection experience to sustain it. They experienced the resurrection, then went out into the world to tell about it. Whether we are convinced or not, they were.

CLARENCE W. CRANFORD

363. RESURRECTION WITHIN THE SOUL

There are men in whom the resurrection begun makes the Resurrection credible. In them the Spirit of the risen Saviour works already; and they have mounted with Him from the grave. They have risen out of the darkness of doubt, and are expatiating in the brightness and the sunshine of a Day in which God is ever Light. Their step is as free as if the clay of the sepulchre had been shaken off; and their hearts are lighter than those of other men; and there is in them an unearthly triumph which they are unable to express. They have risen above the narrowness of life, and all that is petty, and ungenerous, and mean. They have risen above fear—they have risen above self. In the New Testament that is called the spiritual resurrection, a being "risen with Christ": and the man in whom all that is working has got something more blessed than external evidence to rest upon. He has the witness in himself: he has not seen, and yet he has believed: he believes in a resurrection, because he has the Resurrection in himself. The Resurrection in all its heavenliness and unearthly elevation has begun within his soul, and he knows as clearly as if he had demonstration, that it must be developed in an Eternal Life.

FREDERICK W. ROBERTSON

364. ESSENTIAL CHRISTIANITY

Our faith in the resurrection is far more—indeed, radically other—than acceptance of the ancient accounts of Jesus' appearances to his disciples. There is no reason to reject these accounts. However one may conceive of the psychological character of these experiences, there can be no doubt that they occurred. But such experiences by themselves prove nothing: they may be explained in purely subjective terms. As a matter of fact, we are certain to explain them so unless we ourselves "know him and the power of his resurrection" (Phil. 3:10). But if we do thus know him, we cease to have *a priori* either any ground for doubting the objective character of the appearances as such or any imperious reason for maintaining it. For if our faith in the resurrection has any vitality or validity, it is nothing less than the conviction that

175

there is even now present and knowable within the Christian fellowship through "the Holy Spirit, which is given unto us," the full concrete personal meaning of "Jesus Christ and him crucified." This is a mystery—yea, a miracle—but to deny it means denying not only what is essential and central in the Christian theological position but also what has been for twenty centuries the most intimate and secure conviction of Christian devotion. No one can hope to understand the New Testament or the early church who begins by assuming that this conviction was mistaken. The early church's knowledge of the living Christ cannot be separated, except by the most arbitrary procedures, from its knowledge of the crucified Jesus. The same person who was remembered was known still.

JOHN KNOX

365. NEW LIFE

Let those who will explain the how of the resurrection. I have never tried to explain it. In the end all explanations fail. But take away the resurrection, however it happened, and the whole history of Christianity collapses. We dwell in a rational world, a world in which divers truths which we know are true remain unexplained. Great results have great causes, and we are sure that somewhere between the crucifixion and the first preaching of the disciples something happened that entirely changed that group of frightened men. Not only did it change them, but it changed the whole history of the world. The evidence for the resurrection is not so much that we read the account of it in the Gospels, as what we find transpired in the disciples—a new life. At sight of the Cross they ran away. A few weeks later they are found rejoicing to be beaten, imprisoned and put to death. Some of their performances—their quarreling, their divisions, and the strange theologies which the early Church wove about the person of Jesus— may all seem irrelevant to the manner in which Jesus set about to be the doer and achiever of something far greater than the mind of the theologian conceived. Nevertheless, if the Gospel stops with the crucifixion, then God remains unexplained, and the story ends in tragedy.

FREDERICK K. STAMM

366. ULTIMATE OPTIMISM

The resurrection means that the worst has been met and has been conquered. This puts an ultimate optimism at the heart of things. The resurrection says that no matter how life may seem to go to pieces around you, nevertheless, the last word is in love. And that on the plane of the physical, in the here and now. Had it been a spiritual resurrection only, it would have meant that the victory is beyond matter, not in the midst of it. But as the battle was an embodied battle, so the victory is an embodied victory. This sweeps the whole horizon, and says that here and now man can meet and conquer anything—everything. No wonder the Christian in the midst of a decaying order is no pessimist. He has solid grounds for his optimism. He has got hold of unconquered and unconquerable Life.

E. Stanley Jones

367. GOSPEL EMPHASES

A great scholar, in treating of the resurrection, points out the different features emphasised in the accounts of the four evangelists. Matthew dwells chiefly on the *majesty and glory* of the resurrection. Mark insists upon it as a *fact*. Luke treats it as a *spiritual necessity;* and John, as a *touchstone of character*.

George H. Morrison

368. KINSHIP WITH THE RESURRECTION

"It is one of the greatest principles of Christianity," said Pascal, "that that which happened in Jesus Christ may happen in the soul of every Christian," and if the Christian faith has affinities with Calvary today, it also has a kinship with the Resurrection. For through the life and death and resurrection of his Lord the Christian finds the assurance that man is not sailing in a rudderless craft, that he is not riding in a driverless car, that the heart of the universe is sound, and that the future of the universe is safe. He finds the confidence that although evil often builds mighty bulwarks, God always tears them down. He finds the faith that although goodness often seems to speak in nothing but the still, small voice which is neither heard nor heeded, God makes of it at last a trumpet drowning out the roar of the thunder of wrong. The Christian gospel means that history is in God's hands. He can be delayed, but he cannot be defeated, and in his own good time he rolls back the stones from the doors of the man-made tombs of the world and raises from the dead the saviors of mankind

Roy Pearson

F. EVENING AT EMMAUS

369. THE ROAD TO EMMAUS

Twilight. And on a dusty ribboned way,
Out from Jersualem, two travelers walked.
Gray shadows touched their feet, but deeper lay
The shadows in their hearts. They softly talked
Of days just passed, of hopeless days in view,
Of boats, of nets, the while their eyes were dim,
Of Galilee, the work they used to do;
Their voices often stilled, remembering Him.

A stranger also walked that way, and when
They sensed his nearness, some new sympathy
Assuaged their grief. Old hopes came warm again
As, in the dusk, he kept them company . . .
Thus, through the troubled twilight of today
Emmaus road has stretched its shining thread,
And still Christ walks beside men on the way,
To hold the light of hope, to break the bread.

Ida Norton Munson

370. EMMAUS DISCIPLES

Who were these two disciples? Luke names one of them, Cleopas, a shorter form of Cleopatrus, the masculine form of the name we are better acquainted with in the feminine, Cleopatra. We know nothing more of him than we are told in this narrative. Many conjectures have been made as to the identity of the other unnamed disciple. Seven times Origen calls his name Simon, but whether he intended Simon Peter or Simon the Cananaean or Simon (Simeon) later "bishop" of Jerusalem no one can tell. Three times Ambrose names these two disciples as Cleophas and Amaon or Ammaon, the latter name possibly being a corruption of Emmaus as Resch thinks or of Simon as Zahn and Rohrbach think. Epiphanius calls the unnamed disciple Nathaniel, but gives no reason for this decision. Zimmermann suggested James, and Volkmar Paul! Could anything be more absurd than that? Possibly it would be well for us to follow the suggestion of one of the older commentators who said, "The learned cannot come to any agreement who the other disciple was, and I will give you this good counsel—Let each of you take his place."

DOREMUS A. HAYES

371. AT EMMAUS

They knew Him when He broke the bread:
Was it by the accompanying words He said
Which faith, though faltering, understands?
Or wounded beauty of His hands?

CHARLES L. O'DONNELL

372. THEY KNEW THEIR COMPANION

He revealed Himself in the breaking of the bread, and it seems like an anti-climax, does it not? After all this marshalled preparation, shall we not look for something far more glorious? We shall have some vision that will strike the senses? We shall have some flash of glory on the eye? "And He revealed Himself in the breaking of the bread." It was in no sense a sacramental meal, as we use that word sacrament in our theology. It was a frugal supper in a village home of two tired travellers, and another. Yet it was then—in the breaking of the bread, and not in any vision of resurrection splendour—that they knew that their companion was the Lord. How that discovery flashed upon their hearts, the Bible, so wonderful in its silences, does not tell. It may have been the quiet air of majesty with which He took at once the place of host, when they had invited Him in to be their guest. It may have been the familiar word of blessing that awakened sweet memories of Galilean days. Or it may have been that as He put forth His hand after the blessing to take the bread and break it, they saw that it was a hand which had been pierced. However it was, whether by word or hand, they felt irresistibly that this was He. Some little action, some dear familiar trait, told them in a flash that this was the Christ. Not in some vision of resurrection-glory, but in some characteristic movement of the fingers, maybe, they recognized that they found their Lord.

GEORGE H. MORRISON

373. EMMAUSWARD

Lord Christ, if thou art with us and these eyes
Are holden, while we go sadly and say,
"We hoped it had been He, and now to-day
Is the third day, and hope within us dies,"
Bear with us, oh our Master, thou art wise
And knowest our foolishness; we do not pray,
"Declare thyself, since weary grows the way
And faith's new burden hard upon us lies."
Nay, choose thy time; but ah! whoe'er thou art
Leave us not; where have we heard any voice
Like thine? Our hearts burn in us as we go;
Stay with us; break our bread; so, for our part
Ere darkness falls haply we may rejoice,
Haply when day has been far spent may know.

EDWARD DOWDEN

374. LOCATING EMMAUS

Although it is only seven and one-half miles from Jerusalem to Emmaus, the distance that day was an eternity, for modern science has not yet invented an instrument which can measure empty hearts. Where is there a map which marks the spot where hungry and thirsty souls are satisfied? Where is there an artist who can find beauty in a

universe which has lost its Christ? Cleophas and his friends had come
to a dead end.

HAROLD E. WAGNER

G. EVER-LIVING LORD

375. HE MEETS US EVERY DAY

We crucified Him, but God raised Him from the dead. He is risen.
He has overcome the powers of sin and death. A new life has begun.
And in His risen and ascended power, He has sent forth into the
world a new community, bound together by His Spirit, sharing His
divine life, and commissioned to make Him known throughout the
world. He will come again as Judge and King to bring all things to
their consummation. Then we shall know Him as He is and be known
as we are known. Together with the whole creation we wait for this
with eager hope, knowing that God is faithful and that even now He
holds all things in His hand. . . . We do not know what is coming to us.
But we know who is coming. It is He who meets us every day and
who will meet us at the end—Jesus Christ our Lord.

THE EVANSTON REPORT

376. CHRIST OUR CONTEMPORARY

The proclamation of the Christian evangelist is the proclamation of
this Presence. It is an invitation to an encounter where faith can meet
the risen Christ. *To live in a world where Christ is risen is to live in
a world where Christ is our contemporary:* contemporary, not only in
the sense that he is never out of date, but in the sense that he is here.
We live contemporaneously with him.

DANIEL T. NILES

377. CINQUIN: I TOO WAS BORN

When Christ
Arose that morn

181

And walked into the dawn,
Bringing new hope to all, I too
Was born.

HAROLD A. SCHULZ

378. SUMMIT OF THE HILL

W. Y. Fullerton tells of climbing the mimic Calvary of the village of
Domodossola in northern Italy. In ascending order up the hillside a
series of chapels had been built, each depicting, with life-size terra-
cotta figures, one of the scenes of Jesus' Passion—Jesus before Pilate,
Jesus shouldering the cross, and so on. The climax was reached with
the chapel that showed Jesus hanging on the cross, and up to this point
the path running between the shrines was well worn by the feet of
countless pilgrims, come to look upon their Lord's sufferings and
death. But now the path became grassgrown and was clearly little
used. Dr. Fullerton, however, followed on, and, reaching the summit of
the hill, found there another shrine, the Chapel of the Resurrection,
which few, it was clear, took the trouble to visit. Those who built that
mimic Calvary had not forgotten that Jesus rose from the tomb, but
most of the pilgrims came to pay homage to a Christ who, so far as
they were concerned, was dead.

JAMES MARTIN

379. ETERNAL PRINCIPLE

An intricate doctrine has been built up by theologians concerning
the part played in the epic of creation by the Son of God before he
appeared among men as Jesus of Nazareth.

The author of the Fourth Gospel says that "all things were made
through him" (John 1:3), and Luke, the author of Acts, seems to
subscribe to that idea when he quotes Peter as calling him "the Author
of life" (Acts 3:15). Jesus once called himself "the way, the truth, and
the life" (John 14:6). But one does not need to become involved in
theological abstractions in so thinking of Jesus. History will grant him
the title "Author of life."

That there was an eternal principle in him is evident from the Resurrection. It is not merely that men by the hundreds testified that they had seen him alive following the Crucifixion, but that men by the millions down through nineteen centuries have also testified that he was alive in them.

Roy L. Smith

380. FLOWING STREAM

If Christ is a living Christ, as we believe, the Cross can never be merely a past event. It is not shut off in history. Legends enshrine the facts of ultimate human need, and often hint the answer. Thus the legend of the princess who flung herself into an open grave that drought might no longer parch the fields of her people: a stream flowed from the sacrificial grave. Only God could overcome the drought of human sin, and He only by Self-giving. But His Cross and Grave are not past fact, but a fountainhead in very truth. Calvary is not an inert "piece of history"; by His regnant Presence it is a flowing stream. It is cleansing and life in every generation.

George A. Buttrick

381. AND HE WAS ONLY THIRTY-THREE

And He was only thirty-three . . .
The year had come to spring—
And He hung dead upon a tree,
Robbed of its blossoming.
Sorrow of sorrows that Youth should die
On a dead tree 'neath an April sky.

And He was only thirty-three . . .
Anthems of joy be sung—
For, always, the Risen Christ will be
A God divinely young.
Glory of glories, a Tree, stripped bare,
Shed now Faith's blossoms everywhere.

Violet Alleyn Storey

382. *FROM* WHEN THE DAYLIGHT WANES

No more in Galilee we look for Thee,
  O Risen Lord;
In every land and on each moonlit sea
  Thy voice is heard;
And when Thy saints are gathered in Thy Name,
Closer Thou art to each than fire to flame.

THOMAS TIPLADY

383. CHRISTUS CONSUMMATOR

Let us not forget that the last maps will always be made in heaven. You who serve Jesus Christ serve not One who is merely "Christus Consolator"—one who consoles us in our defeats. We also salute and worship "Christus Consummator"—the One who will consummate and finish what He has begun. There is no defeat with Jesus of Nazareth. His Kingdom shall spread from shore to shore, and happy are you, my friends, if you have a part in this one deathless movement and fellowship of history.

LOUIS H. EVANS

384. VIA LUCIS

And have the bright immensities
  Received our risen Lord
Where light-years frame the Pleiades
  And point Orion's sword?

Do flaming suns His footsteps trace
  Through corridors sublime,
The Lord of interstellar space
  And Conqueror of time?

The heaven that hides Him from our sight
  Knows neither near nor far:
An altar candle sheds its light
  As surely as a star;

And where His loving people meet
To share the gift divine
There stands He with unhurrying feet;
There heavenly splendors shine.

HOWARD CHANDLER ROBBINS

H. UNTO A LIVELY HOPE

385. SPRING BELONGS WITH EASTER

Spring itself is Resurrection!
Bough and bud combine to prove
That death is a temporal imperfection
Through which all of Life must move.

From the husk new green arises,
From the kernel roots appear,
And though our hopes wear dark disguises,
Faith can find its white robes here.

RALPH W. SEAGER

386. "IF A MAN DIE, SHALL HE LIVE AGAIN?"

I will repudiate the lie
Men tell of life;
How it will pass
As fragile flower, or butterfly,
Whose dust shall nourish
April grass.

Since one, for love, died on a tree
And in the stony
Tomb was lain,
Behold I show a mystery:
All sepulchres
Are sealed in vain!

JOHN RICHARD MORELAND

185

387. POWER OF AN ENDLESS LIFE

Once we see that Jesus was the greatest, the most original, the most creative, the most dynamic of spiritual personalities, the facts recorded of Him are not only intelligible, but luminous. What men call miracles are but the graceful gestures of such a Being, bearing witness to the divinity of Spirit as creator, repairer, and master of matter. In such a history the story of the Resurrection may seem wonderful—as, indeed, it is—but, none the less, as natural as the blooming of a flower or the shining of a star, since even outside that history we can see no limit to the power of spirit. Jesus did not create faith in immortality: the path of early history is marked by the monuments of forgotten peoples, who left nothing but proofs of their faith in a future life. Jesus revealed Eternal Life. What was before a guess, or at best a hope, He revealed to be a fact by the power of spirit; a power that gives immortality its true character and shows it to be an ever more and more abundant life. Once for all, victoriously, by the power of an endless life, He revealed

> That life is ever lord of death,
> And love can never lose its own.

Joseph Fort Newton

388. FACTS THAT INFLUENCE

Two great ideas are involved in the fact of the Resurrection—ideas influencing human thought and action at every turn—ideas coextensive in their application with human life itself.

First, by opening out the vista of an endless future, it has wholly changed the proportion of things. The capacity of looking forward is the measure of progress in the individual and in the race. Providence is God's attribute. In proportion as a man appropriates this attribute of God, in proportion as his faculty of foresight is educated, in the same degree is he raised in the moral scale. The civilised man is distinguished from the barbarian by the development of this faculty. The barbarian lives only for the day; if he has food and shelter for the moment, he thinks of nothing more. The civilised man forecasts the needs of the future; lays up stores for the future; makes plans for the future. The Christian again is an advance upon the civilised man, as the civilised man was an advance upon the barbarian. His vista of knowledge and interest is not terminated abruptly by the barrier of the grave. The Resurrection has stimulated the faculty and educated the habit of foresight indefinitely, by opening out of it an endless field of vision, over which its sympathies range.

But secondly, the Resurrection involves another principle, not less extensive or less potent in its influence on human life. The Resurrection does not merely proclaim immortality. There would have been no need of Christ's death for that. It declares likewise that death leads to life. It assures us that death is the portal to eternity. Thus it glorifies death; it crowns and consecrates the grave. What is the message of the Risen Christ—the Alpha and Omega—to His Churches? Not merely "I am He that liveth." This was a great fact, but this was not all. Read on. "I am He that liveth, and I was dead." Death issuing in life —death the seed, and life the plant and blossom and fruit—this is the great lesson of the Gospel.

JOSEPH B. LIGHTFOOT

389. *FROM* THE KEY

The Cross of Calvary
Was verily The Key
By which our Brother Christ
Unlocked The Door
Of Immortality
To you and me;
And, passing through Himself before,
He set it wide
For evermore,
That we, by His grace justified,
And by His great love fortified,
Might enter in all fearlessly,
And dwell for ever by His side.

JOHN OXENHAM

390. GLORIFIED PERSONALITY

If we judged by most of the Easter sermons we have heard and read, we would conclude that the idea of the immortality of the soul has almost displaced the preaching of the resurrection. Many people even assume that they are the same thing. This is a serious misconception, and Easter is a good occasion for dispelling it.

Immortality receives its classical expression in Greek philosophy. It implies that there is a radical separation between soul and body, and that at death the soul, freed from its earthly prison-house, continues to exist in a disembodied state.

Resurrection, on the other hand, which is the distinctive view of the New Testament, is something else. It assumes that body and spirit are united in a vital personal whole and that man does not exist apart from a body of some kind. It therefore holds that what we experience after death is not a shadowy continuance in a spirit-world but a glorified personality in a new creation (Rom. 8:18-23 and 1 Cor. 15:20-26).

SAMUEL McCREA CAVERT

391. THE SPIRIT TRIUMPHS

Our chief concern on any Easter day is not so much that we should have unmistakable proof of our immortality, or of the resurrection of Jesus, but our question ought to be, what difference does belief in immortality make to us in our everyday life? After all, we are not angels. We are living in a world of tragedy. We are human beings with all the limitations that our humanness implies; we are living in a world where good is, and where evil threatens us on every hand. We could get out of the world by means of suicide. But most of us do not want to do that, we prefer to live. And so long as we prefer to live, we seek a means whereby we can make the human spirit triumph over all the forces set to defeat it. It is not so much a question as to whether we can believe in miraculous events, but rather whether we can believe in a moral miracle which can happen within us to lift us above the exigencies of life and to inspire others with the same belief.

FREDERICK K. STAMM

IX. Lenten and Easter Worship

A. LENT

1. Calls to Worship and Opening Sentences

392.

Since then we have a great high priest who has passed through the heavens, Jesus, the Son of God, let us hold fast our confession. . . . Let us then with confidence draw near to the throne of grace, that we may receive mercy and find grace to help in time of need. (HEB. 4:14, 16 R.S.V.)

393.

Rend your hearts and not your garments.
Return to the Lord, your God,
    for he is gracious and merciful,
slow to anger, and abounding in steadfast love.

The sacrifice acceptable to God is a broken spirit;
    a broken and contrite heart, O God, thou wilt not despise.

Let us test and examine our ways,
    and return to the Lord!
Let us lift up our hearts and hands
    to God in heaven. (JOEL 2:13; Ps. 51:17; LAM. 3:40-41 R.S.V.)

394.

Let us run with perseverance the race that is set before us, looking to Jesus the pioneer and perfecter of our faith, who for the joy that was set before him endured the cross, despising the shame, and is seated at the right hand of the throne of God. (Heb. 12:1-2 R.S.V.)

395.

[Jesus said], "I am the vine, you are the branches. He who abides in me, and I in him, he it is that bears much fruit, for apart from me you can do nothing. . . . As the Father has loved me, so have I loved you; abide in my love. . . . These things I have spoken to you, that my joy may be in you, and that your joy may be full." (JOHN 15:5, 9, 11 R.S.V.)

2. *Invocations*

396.

O God, whose blessed Son did fast forty days and nights in preparation for his holy mission; beget in us, we beseech thee, the same desire which was in him to learn and do thy will. Forbide that through indulgence of the flesh we should dim our vision of thee and render ourselves unfit for thy service. Give us grace to master our bodies and bring them into subjection to thy good purpose for us. Teach us by prayer and fasting to win self-control, that we may count ourselves wholly to thee and enter more and more into thy blessed kingdom; through him who for our sake consecrated himself, Jesus Christ our Lord.

ERNEST FREMONT TITTLE

397.

O Thou living God, our Father, who art ever more ready to give than we to ask, Thou to whom the things are possible that are impossible to us, grant us to-day, we beseech Thee, a new vision of Thyself, that seeing Thee as Thou art, in Thy majesty, in Thy holiness, in Thy compassionate and understanding love, we may desire Thee, and, desiring Thee, may surrender to Thee, and, surrendering to Thee, body, soul, and spirit, without reserve, may find our lives transformed by Thy Creative Spirit into the likeness of Jesus Christ. For Thy name's sake we ask it.

WILLIAM ADAMS BROWN

398.

O Lord Jesus Christ, who art the image of the invisible God, and who speakest to us the words of eternal life, who for our sake didst give Thyself to the death upon the Cross, in whom we trust, and on whom our hope is staid; pardon our sins, we beseech thee, for Thy tender mercy's sake. Help us to understand and to be understood by our fellowmen; to be victorious in our warfare against evil; and to accomplish every task which Thou mayest set us; open the door of heaven that we may see Thy glory; fit us for the resurrection life in the world to come, and grant us that peace which passeth all understanding; who livest and reignest with the Father and the Holy Spirit, one God, world without end.

J. WILSON SUTTON

399.

O God, we thank Thee for this life, with all its joys, its opportunities, its discipline. But we could scarcely thank Thee for this life had we no hope of a better, in which all we here learn may be used, and in which all we have here loved may be fully enjoyed. Increase our faith, and give us a more lively apprehension of the reality of things unseen, a firmer assurance that life is not a vain and fruitless spending of time, that there is a purpose in it, the attainment of which will justify all toil, and sacrifice, and thought, and feeling.

MARCUS DODS

3. Prayers

400.

O God of grace and glory, Thou art to us like sunrise ending the night, like the surrounding hills ever present in quiet strength, like music inviting the heart to peace and joy.

Forgive when in stupidity we have been blind to Thy majesty, deaf to Thy voice, indifferent to Thy purpose. May the dignity of reverence and the freedom of obedience ennoble us.

Strengthen now, we pray, desire to love and serve Thee. May awareness of Thy Presence be a companion to every thought and confidence in Thy saving power our highway to life.

During these days of the Lenten pilgrimage, grant us grace to trace the footprints of Jesus Christ and be captured by His spirit. Clothe us with the garments of His humility, empower us with the dynamic of His Faith, direct us by the intelligence of his love, and sound the trumpets of His courage in our hearts.

So may we fulfill the purpose for which we were born and, as those whom Christ would call friends, release in the world the healing goodness for which it waits.

EVERETT W. PALMER

401.

O Thou brave Son of Man,
Who learned by all Thou sufferedst how to obey,
Teach us, Thy lesser brothers,
The meaning of the will of God
In this our troublous day.
Thou hast promised
That if any man would do the Father's will
He shall have light.
Out of weakness and irresolution we claim that promise.
Share with us some measure of Thy valor
That we may do our Father's will.
Come Thou to us, O Lord,
In every storm of temptation,
In every tedious stretch of work,
In every day of doubt,
In every night of suffering,
Remind, empower and direct us.
We would believe,
Help Thou our unbelief;
Remember no more our false pretense,
And enable us to find our freedom
In obedience unto Thee.

GEORGE STEWART

402.

Jesus, the Crucified, when I must walk the way which Thou hast
trod, go Thou with me.
In the wilderness of temptation, fortify me.
From the standards of the world, release me.
In the waters of renewal, cleanse me.
At the place of witness, inspire me.
In the hour of decision, guide me.
In the darkness of sorrow, console me.
On the mountain of vision, transform me.
At the table of love, nourish me.
In the garden of betrayal, comfort me.
At the court of earthly judgment, support me.

At the pillar of scourging, strengthen me.
On the way of suffering, uplift me.
On the cross of sacrifice, accept me.
From the tomb of death, raise me.
At the throne of grace, crown me.
In the mansions of heaven, give me life and peace with Thee forever.

G. A. CLEVELAND SHRIGLEY

B. PASSION SUNDAY

1. Calls to Worship and Opening Sentences

403.
While we were yet helpless, at the right time Christ died for the un-
godly. . . . God shows his love for us in that while we were yet sinners
Christ died for us. . . . As Christ was raised from the dead by the
glory of the Father, we too [must] walk in newness of life. (ROM. 5:6,
8; 6:4 R.S.V.)

404.
Have this mind among yourselves, which you have in Christ Jesus,
who . . . humbled himself and became obedient unto death, even
death on a cross. Therefore God has highly exalted him and bestowed
on him the name which is above every name, that at the name of Jesus
every knee should bow, in heaven and on earth and under the earth,
and every tongue confess that Jesus Christ is Lord, to the glory of
God the Father. (PHIL. 2:2, 8-11)

405.
Grace to you and peace from God the Father and our Lord Jesus
Christ, who gave himself for our sins to deliver us from the present
evil age, according to the will of our God and Father; to whom be
the glory for ever and ever. (GAL. 1:3-5 R.S.V.)

2. Invocations

406.
O Saviour, who didst set Thy face as a flint to go to Jerusalem to
Thy Cross and Passion, help us, Thy weak and wavering disciples, to

193

be firm and resolute in the path of duty. We confess that we have refused to share the burden of Thy Cross, that we have denied Thee rather than face mockery, and have sought comfort and security rather than the doing of Thy will. Forgive our sin, help us to amend, and give us courage to endure worthily; for Thy Name's sake.

DAVID A. MacLENNAN

407.

O Eternal God, out of the darkness which enfolds Thee has appeared a light, and out of the silence in which Thou dwellest has sounded a voice, so that Thou art no longer all unknown to us, Thy creatures. The face of Jesus is Thy light, and the Cross of Jesus is Thy voice. Grant that I may so meditate upon the life of Jesus, and so enter into the fellowship of His sacrifice, that I may apprehend Thee as Thou truly art, holy and compassionate, righteous and loving towards sinners; and knowing Thee in Thy Son, may give to Thee the offering which Thou desirest, even myself to be Thy servant; through Jesus Christ our Lord.

W. R. MATTHEWS

408.

Almighty God, whose only-begotten Son was lifted up from the earth: give us grace, we humbly beseech thee, to seek only the gain of sacrifice, and to strive only for the exaltation of service; that so we may be drawn unto him who by his cross and precious blood hath redeemed us, our Lord and Saviour Jesus Christ.

JOHN WALLACE SUTER

3. Prayers

409.

Almighty God, who knowest the weaknesses which we are slow to confess even to ourselves, take from us, we beseech Thee, the faithless mind that would shrink from the way by which Thou leadest, and draw back from the hard paths of a dutiful life. As disciples of the Man of Sorrows, may we steadfastly set our face to go to Jerusalem, prepared to meet all the counsels of Thy will and to be obedient even unto death, seeking only for strength to glorify the cross Thou layest upon us. Help us to cast out of the temple of our hearts everything which in our moments of clear and solemn vision we know ought not to be there—every temper and passion and desire that cannot bear the searching scrutiny of divine purity and love. O God, dwell in us more and more: dwell in our minds as truth, in our hearts as love, in our wills as strength, and nevermore leave Thy temple.

JOHN HUNTER

410.

O Thou Eternal God, who in Thy Son Jesus Christ hast come among men to suffer and die for our redemption, we lift our hearts to Thee. To Thee be glory and majesty, dominion and power, even as in Thee are mercy, forgiveness and never-failing love.

We lift to Thee grateful hearts for the life, the ministry, the gracious words, the holy and loving acts of Jesus. In Him have men of every time and place found a way of life, and a way to life. By His life have our lives been judged, challenged, guided, and made new in a peace that passes understanding. We thank Thee, O God.

Above all, O God, we thank Thee that He loved us enough to suffer and to die for us. Our little minds cannot fathom the mystery of such love, or understand its power. Yet we know that in the death of Christ for our redemption we see Thee in Thy fulness; we lay hold in wonder and gratitude upon Thy supreme self-giving. At Thy behest Christ died for us, and that is all we need to know. We yield ourselves to Thee in adoration and glad obedience.

Yet as we think upon the greatness of Thy gift, we confess in penitence before Thee the littleness of our faith and love. Thou hast called us to service in love of Thee and our fellow men, and we have followed too much the impulses of self-will. Thou hast called us to trust in Thee, and in self-trust and self-despair our lives have been cluttered with anxieties. Thou hast called us to hope, and we have lived as those who have no hope. Forgive us, good Lord.

We pray Thee, O God, to create in us clean hearts and to renew a right spirit within us. When we fail, give us courage; when we are proud, make us humble; when we are self-seeking, increase our love; when we are indifferent to Thee and to the world's great need, help us to care. Strengthen us now, we pray.

What we ask for ourselves we ask for all Thy children. Let those who are hungry in body or soul be fed. Let those who are sick be made well, those who are downcast be lifted up. Give courage to the fearful, strength to the weak, and a new spirit to those who feel rancor or hate. Let Thy way be made known upon the earth, Thy saving health among all nations. We pray alike for our friends and our enemies, and bid Thee stir in us such friendliness that enmities may cease. Let our evil be overcome with good, O Lord.

And so we commit ourselves to Thee for the doing of Thy will. As our Lord has suffered for us, so let us walk His way of the cross. Not in boasted martyrdoms or self-pity, but in humble dedication to Thy will, we would suffer as Thou callest us to do. And may our suffering be a pathway to Thy service, our self-glorying be lost in Thy infinite glory. Use us, O Lord, as Thou desirest, and with Thee we will leave the fruitage of our labor.

All this we pray in the name of Him who is forever the Way, the Truth and the Life.

GEORGIA HARKNESS

411.

O God, who in the death of thy beloved Son didst endure for our sake the agony of the cross; grant to us, we beseech thee, such a measure of thy Spirit that we may not shrink from loss or pain in thy service but may do all we can under thee to help one another and to promote justice and peace upon earth. Forbid that we should complain of burdens and ills that are not worthy to be compared with the sufferings of Christ or the wounds of many among his faithful disciples. Save us from the weakness and futility of self-pity, and from faithless brooding and anxiety. Give us grace to forget ourselves in concern for others. Teach us to find healing for our hurt in unwearied effort to heal the hurt of the world. Fill us with thine own compassion for the sick, the hungry, the lonely, the discouraged, and for all who are victims of prejudice and injustice, that we may enter into the constancy and joy of thy service, and be able to comfort those who are in any affliction with the comfort wherewith we ourselves are comforted of thee; through Jesus Christ our Lord.

ERNEST FREMONT TITTLE

C. PALM SUNDAY

1. Calls to Worship and Opening Sentences

412.

Rejoice greatly, O daughter of Zion!
  Shout aloud, O daughter of Jerusalem!
Lo, your king comes to you;
  triumphant and victorious is he, humble and riding on an ass,
  on a colt the foal of an ass.
The kingdom of the world has become the kingdom of our Lord
and of his Christ, and he shall reign for ever and ever. (Zech. 9:9-10;
Rev. 11:15 R.S.V.)

413.

Lift up your heads, O gates!
  and be lifted up, O ancient doors!
  that the King of glory may come in.
Who is the King of glory?
  The Lord, strong and mighty,
  the Lord, mighty in battle!
Lift up your heads, O gates!
  and be lifted up, O ancient doors!
  that the King of glory may come in!
Who is this King of glory?
  The Lord of hosts,
  he is the King of glory! (Ps. 24:7-10 R.S.V.)

414.

A great crowd who had come to the feast heard that Jesus was coming
to Jerusalem. So they took branches of palm trees and went out to meet
him, crying, "Hosanna! Blessed be he who comes in the name of the
Lord, even the King of Israel!" (John 12:12-13 R.S.V.)

415.

Get you up to a high mountain,
  O Zion, herald of good tidings;
lift up your voice with strength,

197

O Jerusalem, herald of good tidings,
lift it up, fear not;
say to the cities of Judah, "Behold your God!" (Isa. 40:9 R.S.V.)

2. *Invocations*

416.

Almighty God, we who know the bondage of fear celebrate today
the invincible joy of Jesus Christ our Lord. The sight of him, humble
but unswerving, entering the city of darkest hate, holding the gift of
gladness from little children against the priest's complaint, unafraid
of the fate of death, as though all this were his day's work, redeems us
from our own cowardice and confusion. Grant us too the triumph of
the soul's joy against the empty pleasure of the world's applause,
through Jesus Christ.

SAMUEL H. MILLER

417.

O God, whose dearly beloved Son was greeted by the crowd on Olivet
with halleluiahs, but who in that same week was mocked as he went
lonely to the cross, forbid that our welcome of him should be in words
alone. Help us, we beseech thee, to keep the road open for him into
our hearts; and let him find there not another crucifixion, but love and
loyalty in which his kingdom may be established evermore.

WALTER RUSSELL BOWIE

418.

Heavenly Father, make of this day the time of heart-searching for us.
As we rejoice in the triumphal entry of Christ, may we become instru-
ments of Thine in working out the means of salvation for all people.
Bless our efforts as they are united with those of Christians throughout
the world. May Thy Kingdom come into our lives as we accept Him.
Make us triumphant through His humility and unselfish sacrifice.

JOHN LEWIS SANDLIN

419.

Our Father, gladly have we come to the mount that is called Olivet;
here would we too make ready for the triumphant entry of our

Master. Lead us into the secrets of gracious quiet and serene spiritual loveliness, that with joyful self-abandonment we may swell the chorus of Thy children who this day proclaim Jesus anew as Lord of lords and King of kings.

HERMAN PAUL GUHSÉ

3. Prayers

420.

Almighty God, our Heavenly Father, we come into Thy presence this day with reverence and true adoration in our spirits. We honor Thee through Christ as the King of our lives. We praise Thee for Thy power. We find life's deep content made secure in Thy love, and we are happy to rejoice in Thine everlasting mercy.

We would join our voices with the throngs across the ages who on this day have honored Christ the King. We would open our hearts that He may reign there, rule over our thoughts and our needs, our intentions and our desires, and all the surging vitalities of our nature, until all things are made subject to Him and to His Lordship. Wilt Thou bless this congregation gathered here in the spirit of worship and faith, and may that blessing be a means of bringing life up to new levels of faith and courage and understanding.

LOWELL M. ATKINSON

421.

O God, Ruler of the universe, Lord of all power, and King of our souls; we praise thee for thy Son, Jesus Christ, who brought thy reign of love and righteousness for every age. Thou openest the gates of beauty and of truth. Thanks be unto thee, O Thou who comest to enthrone the hope and spirit of thy kingdom among the multitudes of the world today.

As thou enterest the highway of our hearts, O Christ, we would welcome thee with the branches of adoration and the garments of rejoicing. Let not our devotion to thee turn into timidness and desertion when faith and justice are on trial among us. May we never spurn thine everlasting truth for the false and low standards of the crowd. Forbid that we should try to make thee our kind of king and miss becoming thy kind of followers.

O holy Conqueror of evil, as soldiers of thine make us unafraid of crosses and bravely patient in the slow victories of goodness. Establish us in true greatness of the Christian life, clothed in the stature of humility and strong in love. So may our outward loyalty to thy church be sealed by the homage of consecration, O Saviour, who hast dominion forever and ever.

O Lord, help each of us to become portals of thy entry into the lives about us. While nations shake for fear, steady us in the knowledge that thou art reigning beyond terror and tyranny. Strong Deliverer, come unto all the weary and heavy-laden and bring thy saving freedom to all in bondage of sin and under the yoke of oppression. Bring to us the peace which rises out of the triumph of forgiveness and obedience. Accept our thanksgiving for all thy servants who have been good examples unto us. May all who confirm their faith this day find joy in thy service as heirs of thy kingdom. We hail thee, thou Son of the Highest. Come to our worship and make it a coronation of life as thou, O King of Glory, enterest in. We ask it in thy name which is above every name.

SAMUEL JOHN SCHMIECHEN

422.

O Lord Jesus Christ, who on this day didst enter the rebellious city where Thou wast to die, enter into our hearts we beseech Thee and subdue them wholly to Thyself. And as Thy faithful disciples blessed Thy coming and spread their garments in the way, may we be ready to lay at Thy feet all that we have and are and to bless Thee, O Thou who comest in the name of the Lord. And grant that after having confessed and worshiped Thee upon earth, we may be among the number of those who shall hail Thine eternal triumphs and bear in their hands the palms of victory, when every knee shall bow before Thee and every tongue confess that Thou art Lord and that Thou shalt reign forever and ever.

CLOSET AND ALTAR

423.

Incarnate Son of God, who in the days of thy flesh didst bring life and immortality to light, with all those of all centuries who have loved and trusted thee we sing, "Hosanna in the highest! Blessed is he that cometh in the name of the Lord." Thou art the King of Glory and the Prince of Peace, and to thee we open the portals of our hearts if thou wilt deign to dwell therein. Rule over us in all the concerns and circumstances of our lives: the work of our hands and the whims of our hearts, the ambitions of our desires and the aims of our dreams, the sanctity of our friendships and our attitude toward all mankind. Save us from the hypocrisy that sings "Hosanna" in the temple, and cries "Crucify him" in the market place. Save us from the sham that praises with the lips and betrays in the deed. Deliver us from the treason that boasts loyalty in the upper room, and then makes cowardly denial in the judgment hall. And when the palms have withered, the songs are dead and the streets empty, may we find ourselves at the end of life's little day still with thee, awaiting the eternal sunshine.

WALLACE PETTY

D. MAUNDY THURSDAY

1. Calls to Worship and Opening Sentences

424.

Christ, our paschal lamb, has been sacrificed. Let us, therefore, celebrate the festival, not with the old leaven, the leaven of malice and evil, but with the unleavened bread of sincerity and truth.

To the Lamb be blessing and honor and glory and might for ever and ever. (I COR. 5:7-8; REV. 5:13 R.S.V.)

425.

The bread of God is that which comes down from heaven, and gives life to the world.
The cup of blessing which we bless, is it not a participation in the blood of Christ? The bread which we break, is it not a participation of the body of Christ?
Let a man examine himself, and so eat of the bread and drink of the cup. (JOHN 6:33; I COR. 10:16; 11:28 R.S.V.)

426.

When the hour came, [Jesus] sat at table, and the apostles with him. And he said to them, "I have earnestly desired to eat this passover with

201

you before I suffer; for I tell you I shall not eat it until it is fulfilled in the kingdom of God." (LUKE 22:14-16 R.S.V.)

2. *Invocations*

427.

O Christ of the Passion, who at the Last Supper didst bequeath to the Church a perpetual memorial of the sacrifice of the Cross, help us in this holy Sacrament steadfastly to contemplate Thy redeeming love, that we may ever be mindful of the price wherewith Thou hast bought us; who livest and reignest with the Father and the Holy Ghost, ever one God, world without end.

CHARLES HENRY BRENT

428.

O Almighty God, whose blessed Son did institute and ordain holy mysteries as pledges of his love, and for a continual remembrance of his death; mercifully grant that we and all who shall come to this Holy Table, may be filled with a deep sense of the exceeding holiness of that blessed mystery, and, drawing near with true penitent hearts, and lively faith, in love and charity with all men, may worthily receive that Holy Sacrament, and obtain the fulness of thy grace, to our present comfort and everlasting salvation.

PRAYERS FOR THE CHRISTIAN YEAR

429.

Our Father, the sacred remembrance of Jesus Christ has drawn us into sacramental bonds. Here we would gather about the strong Son of God, amid the glory of His eternal strength and beauty. Here would we freely confess our sins, and prayerfully await Thy pardon, as our hearts are humbled and subdued by unbounded grace and love divine. Out of Thine abundant supply of heavenly treasures grant us perfect peace, complete pardon, unfailing faith, everlasting strength and infinite love.

HERMAN PAUL GUHSÉ

430.

Almighty Father, the strength of all valiant spirits, be thou with us when we are tried to the uttermost. As thou didst strengthen the will of Christ in Gethsemane, and didst walk with him, his unseen comrade, on the road to Calvary, so do thou walk with us on the straight hard road of duty. As we follow the path of sacrifice, grant that we endure hardship as good soldiers of Jesus Christ. Strengthen us by discipline, refine our spirits as by fire, and grant that steadfastly we may set our hearts upon the realities that are eternal.

HENRY HALLAM SAUNDERSON

3. Prayers

431.

O God, who art the giver of every good and perfect gift, for the outpoured life of Jesus Christ we thank thee. So often we have sought to avoid him, yet unfailingly has he followed us and this day comes knocking at our doors.

We praise thee for his fellowship with his disciples on their last night together, for his washing of their feet, for the meal of bread and wine. And this day we gather in his Name, asking thee to take this bread and this cup and to sanctify it to our use and to the advancement of his great kingdom of love.

Our Father, we acknowledge that we have done little to forward the kingdom of Christ. Our feeble hands have hung at our sides. Our minds have been dull and our lives have revealed none of his radiance. Lord God, quicken us, we beseech thee, in our desire to seek first the kingdom of God. Help us to share our great privileges with all mankind. Bless thy church throughout the world. Purify it where it is corrupt. Grant sight where it is blind. Give it a calm abandon in thy Name, where caution rules overmuch its counsels. As it goes forward into its new day of challenge, may it keep faith with its Master. In his Name.

ELMORE MCNEILL MCKEE

432.

O Bread of Life, feed us; Wine of God, refresh us. Grant us, Merciful Lord, by the light of a purified spirit, to attain that which we celebrate in a holy rite. Fed by the Loaf of Fellowship, may we ever hunger after those things by which we truly live. Renewed by the Cup of Sacrifice, may we serve Thee faithfully by a life well pleasing in Thy sight.

O Lamb of God, help Thy servants who drink of the Cup of the New Covenant to become communicants with all who love Thee in sincerity. As we partake of Thy sacraments, may we do it as if from the hand of the Lord Jesus; and may the vision of Him grow and abide until we sit with Him, and with those we love, in the Kingdom of Heaven. In His name.

JOSEPH FORT NEWTON

E. GOOD FRIDAY

1. Calls to Worship and Opening Sentences

433.

Christ also suffered for you, leaving you an example, that you should follow in his steps. He committed no sin; no guile was found on his lips. When he was reviled, he did not revile in return; when he suffered, he did not threaten; but he trusted to him who judges justly. He himself bore our sins in his body on the tree, that we might die to sin and live to righteousness. By his wounds you have been healed. For you were straying like sheep, but have now returned to the Shepherd and Guardian of your souls. (I Pet. 2:21-25 R.S.V.)

434.

[Jesus said], "If any man would come after me, let him deny himself and take up his cross and follow me. For whoever would save his life will lose it, and whosoever loses his life for my sake will find it." (Matt. 16:24-25 R.S.V.)

435.

I, when I am lifted up from the earth, will draw all men to myself. Worthy is the Lamb who was slain, to receive power and wealth and wisdom and might and honor and glory and blessing. (John 12:32; Rev. 5:12 R.S.V.)

436.

Surely he has borne our griefs
and carried our sorrows; yet we esteemed him stricken,

smitten by God and afflicted. But he was wounded for our transgressions,
he was bruised for our iniquities;
upon him was the chastisement that made us whole,
and with his stripes we are healed. (Isa. 53:4-5 R.S.V.)

2. Invocations

437.

Lord Jesus Christ, who for the redemption of mankind didst ascend
the cross, that thou mightest enlighten the world that lay in darkness;
gather us this day with all thy faithful to that same holy cross, that
gazing in penitence upon thy great sacrifice for us, we may be loosed
from all our sins, and entering into the mystery of thy passion, be
crucified to the vain pomp and power of this passing world; and being
counted worthy to suffer with thee here, and finding our glory in
the cross alone, may we attain at last the light eternal, where thou,
the Lamb that once was slain, reignest for ever on the throne of God.

DIVINE SERVICE

438.

O Lord Jesus Christ, the same yesterday, today and forever; O Saviour
of the ever-loving heart; we have grieved and wounded Thee. By our
wilfulness, by our moral cowardice, by our thoughtlessness, by our
self-seeking we share in crucifying Thee afresh. By the revelation Thou
hast made of the eternal love help us to enter into the travail of Thy
soul, and by loving self-sacrifice blend our wills with Thy will to
bring all men to a knowledge of the Father.

AUTHOR UNKNOWN

439.

By the remembrance of the suffering of our Lord Jesus Christ, both
in body and in soul, we present ourselves to thee, prepared in all humility to be subject to the work of thy Holy Spirit, that we may be
purged of pride and vainglory, delivered of double-mindedness and
confusion and rid of every bitterness and hatred. With the confession
of such sins and the cleansing of our hearts, we welcome thee gladly
and with peace, that walking in the way of the Lord we may glorify

thy name by the forgiveness of our enemies and the blessing of all whose ways mingle with ours in the tragic suffering of our world.

SAMUEL H. MILLER

440.

Lord Jesus Christ, thou holy and spotless Lamb of God, who didst take upon thyself our sins, and bear them in thy body on the cross; we bless thee for all the burdens thou hast borne, for all the tears thou hast wept, for all the pains thou hast suffered, for all the words of comfort thou hast spoken from the cross, for all thy conflicts with the powers of darkness, and for thine eternal victory over death and hell. With the host of the redeemed, we ascribe unto thee power and riches and wisdom and strength and honor and glory and blessing, for ever and ever.

G. B. F. HALLOCK

3. Prayers

441.

O God, who hast redeemed us through the mystery of the cross; we bow before thee in reverent gratitude for the revelation of thy love declared in Jesus Christ. We praise thee that he shared our common life and humbled himself and became obedient unto death, even the death of the cross. We bless thee that he bore our griefs, carried our sorrows, and triumphed over sin and death. We glorify thee that through his perfect and sufficient sacrifice on the cross there is pardon for the penitent, power to overcome for the faithful, and transformed life for all who truly turn to him.

Give us grace to yield ourselves in glad surrender to the Lord Jesus. May we share his spirit of obedience to thy will, his consecration to the welfare of humanity, and his passion that thy kingdom may come and thy will be done on earth as it is in heaven. So may Christ dwell in our hearts and reign there as our divine Redeemer.

CARL A. GLOVER

442.

O God who lovest with an everlasting love, and from old hast been afflicted in all Thy children's affliction, bearing them in Thy pity and redeeming them, Thou hast made Thy Word flesh in Jesus, and hast bared Thy heart to us in His cross.

We stand before it, burdened. Lo! this is our world: it slays its best; yea, it is enmity against thee, its God. And these who condemn and crucify Him, are our kinsmen—mind of our mind, spirit of our spirit, Who shall deliver us?

We stand before it amazed. Behold how He loved us! We cannot escape His constraint. We can no longer live unto ourselves.

We stand before it dedicated. Such love is not for us alone, but for a whole world. We dare not keep for ourselves what belongs to our brethren everywhere. Good Shepherd, Thou hast other sheep; them also Thou must bring. And how shall they hear Thy voice except Thy disciples become Thy word for them? We offer ourselves a living sacrifice to fill up on our part that which is lacking in the sufferings of Christ for His Body's sake, the Church.

O Saviour of the world, uplifted that Thou mightest draw all men unto Thee, we bring Thee in tender intercession those who are in pain or sorrow or loneliness, and especially such as are self-imprisoned. Let the heart of God unveiled at Calvary be their comfort and their deliverer. And grant that they and we, and all who have looked upon Thee in Thy passion, may bear the marks of Thy cross upon us, and live in that love which believeth, hopeth, endureth all and never faileth.

HENRY SLOANE COFFIN

443.

O Lord of life, who we remember today as Lord over the powers of tragedy and death, we bow in hushed reverence at the foot of thy cross and listen once more for thy words of eternal life.

Within our awakened minds there falls thy blessing upon those who persecuted you, "Father, forgive them." Not for those who first crowded about thy cross do we pray, O Lord, but for ourselves who in manifold ways have denied thee, ignored thee, and passed thee with an air of casual indifference. We pray that thou wilt forgive us, for we at least are keenly aware of what we have neglected to do and even now continue not to do for thee and thy kingdom.

Lift our hearts upon the wings of radiant faith as we hear thee speak to the anguished and penitent thief, "Today you will be with me in Paradise." How often in divers ways have we prolonged our decision to serve thee in a complete surrender of body, mind and spirit! Yet now at this late hour we claim for ourselves the promise made to him who hung at thy side.

We praise thee for that hallowed moment when, turning to thy mother, thou didst say, "Woman, behold your son," and to thy faithful disciple, "Behold your mother." O Lord, who in thy hour of agony did not forget thine own and whose blessed benediction rests upon our own, we thank thee for the ways by which thy life has bound together in deepening love not only those of our households but our brethren throughout thy world who at this hour are also commending us to thee.

When the shadows lengthen and our spirits become lost in labyrinths of baffling bewilderment, may we hear thy prayer, "My God, my God, why hast thou forsaken me?" O Lord, who wert believing even in that hour of questioning, maintain in us thy courageous conviction that God never abandons his children, but makes clear the paths their feet must follow.

O Christ, as we hear thy words, "I thirst," our hearts become more sensitive to thy love which passeth understanding and to thy stripes by which we are healed. In thy name, O Lord, we dedicate ourselves, all that we are and all we possess, to the nurturing in body and spirit of thy little ones who need to receive from our hands a cup of cold water or a cup of friendly assurance.

As the clouds deepen over Golgotha's rim we hear thy words, "It is finished." With what majestic serenity of spirit thou brought to perfect fruition those ministries of thy Father for the cure of souls, the strengthening of hearts, and the unveiling of eternal truth. Yet, O Lord, how much remains to be done by thy disciples in the proclaiming of thy gospel of salvation and in perfecting our lives through consecrated endeavor!

And now, Lord, as the lingering shadows obscure from thy eyes the world thou didst come to save, we hear thy final word, "Father, into thy hands I commit my spirit." We know once more that thou hast led the way and that all men may triumphantly follow as they return at last to God their home.

CHARLES L. WALLIS

444.

God of the Cross, in what a dark world Thou hast set our lives, where sin and suffering reign and man is saved by the sacrifice of the best.

Yet is the darkness of Thy mystery more revealing than the light of our knowledge; by it we are softened, subdued, and sanctified. In its darkness there is a deeper wisdom; out of its shadow grows our faith for to-day and our hope for the morrow. High truth is here, even the final truth of our life and Thine.

Consider, O Lord, and hear us; slay in us that which slew Jesus on the Cross, even the sin which our sin hides from us by its blindness. Forgive our impure love, our shameless selfishness, our cruel pride, whereby we crucify Him afresh; yea, our hate of those who need our love, and our love of that which Thou hast made us to hate. Let some leaf of the Bitter Tree fall uopn our hearts, that when we suffer for our sins, or are broken by the sins of others, we may suffer in the fellowship of Christ; not in bitterness, but in the beauty of a self-giving love.

Redeem us to Thyself, O God, by the grace of Him whose shame is our glory, whose sorrow is our joy, and whose bitter death is our brightest hope. O Mercy of God, hear our prayer, and return it to us in a quickening of soul to seek more earnestly the purity by which Thou art known, until Thy love is perfected in us; through Jesus, our Lord, who gave Himself for us on the Cross.

JOSEPH FORT NEWTON

F. EASTER

1. Calls to Worship and Opening Sentences

445.

This is the day which the Lord has made;
    let us rejoice and be glad in it.
Christ being raised from the dead will never die again; death no longer has dominion over him.
Rejoice in the Lord always; again I will say, Rejoice. (Ps. 118:24; ROM. 6:9; PHIL. 4:4 R.S.V.)

446.

Do not be afraid; for I know that you seek Jesus who was crucified. He is not here; for he has risen, as he said. Come, see the place where he lay. Then go quickly and tell his disciples that he has risen from the dead, and behold, he is going before you to Galilee; there you will see him. (MATT. 28:5-7 R.S.V.)

447.

If then you have been raised with Christ, seek the things that are above, where Christ is, seated at the right hand of God. Set your minds on things that are above, not on things that are on earth. For you have died, and your life is hid with Christ in God. (COL. 3:1-3 R.S.V.)

448.

[Jesus said], "I am the resurrection and the life; he who believes in me, though he die, yet shall he live, and whoever lives and believes in me shall never die."
He laid his right hand upon me, saying, "Fear not, I am the first and the last, and the living one; I died, and behold I am alive for evermore." (JOHN 11:25-26; REV. 1:17-18 R.S.V.)

449.

Blessed be the God and Father of our Lord Jesus Christ! By his great mercy we have been born anew to a living hope through the resurrection of Jesus Christ from the dead, and to an inheritance which is imperishable, undefiled, and unfading, kept in heaven for you, who by God's power are guarded through faith for a salvation ready to be revealed in the last time. (I PET. 1:3-5 R.S.V.)

2. Invocations

450.

Almighty God, our Father, who art not the God of the dead but of the living, we give Thee joyful thanks this Easter morn for him who is the Resurrection and the Life. We believe in him, in the beauty of his character, and in the triumph of his spirit. Grant that in this sacred hour we may grow aware of him, not as a far-off, blessed memory, but as our eternal Friend and Master who was dead and is alive forevermore. By the power of his resurrection may we rise out of selfishness and sin into a diviner fellowship with Thyself.

JAMES DALTON MORRISON

451.

Almighty and everlasting God, who on Easter Day didst turn the despair of the disciples into triumph by the resurrection of Christ who had been crucified, give us faith to believe that every good which has seemed to be overcome by evil, and every love which has seemed to be buried in darkness and in death, shall rise again in life immortal; through the same Jesus Christ who lives with thee for evermore.

WALTER RUSSELL BOWIE

452.

O risen and victorious Christ, whose power and love destroyed the darkness and death of sin; ascend, we pray thee, the throne of our hearts, and so rule our wills by the might of that immortality wherewith thou hast set us free, that we may evermore be alive unto God, through the power of thy glorious resurrection; world without end.

JOHN WALLACE SUTER

3. Prayers

453.

Unto Thee, O Christ, who has conquered death and risen again, be glory evermore! Light of the World, Splendor of the Father's presence, Son of Man in humility of self-devotion, Son of God in power—Thy risen life is the assurance of our victory. From our low estate—compassed with weakness, made subject to the death of the body—we look up with grateful and exultant hearts to Thee. Thou hast tasted death for every man and risen again from Thy humiliation into glory. As Thou hast called us to be one with Thee in suffering, so lead us through experience of Thy help in trial to the triumph of Thy risen and eternal life. Rid us of all absorbing love of earth and of all bondage to the fear of death. Purify our hearts by the indwelling of Thy Spirit, that we may wait Thy coming with expectant joy. And to God Most High, the God and Father of our Lord Jesus Christ, be praise evermore!

ISAAC O. RANKIN

454.

We come to Thee in the spirit of this day—as children of the Resurrection, who have been begotten again to a lively hope. Help us to live

211

remembering, and loving to remember, Him who died for us and who rose again. May this be to us a day of brightness, of calmness, of joy, of humiliation, of contrition, of holy purpose. We seek to worship Thee in simplicity through Jesus Christ, accepting Him as the image of the Invisible God, the true revealer of Thee the Father. May we enter into that real communion with Him by which we become members of Christ. May we feel this unity to be most real—a unity whose root is love, and therefore the best, which is eternal, and identifies us in all things with Him. Enable us to realise some of the great things which are given to us in this union—the encouragement of knowing we are loved, of being accompanied through life by One who knows the way, and who has Himself triumphed, who lived His life in evidence that the best things can be obtained. Especially He had a life in direct communication with Thee the Father; and this He gives to us—a life forgiven, at peace, an energetic and hopeful fulfilment of God's will.

We desire truly to consecrate ourselves to Thee. Put that heart within us which shall make this true, necessary, abiding.

When disheartened by our own guilt and weakness may we find consolation and renewal in Thee, and may we be enabled to believe that we can be as truly nourished by Christ's life as each member is by the life of the body. And as He embraced all men in His love, and could leave none outside, so may we be emptied of self and filled with love to Thee and to our fellow-men, doing good to all as we have opportunity. In all that we purpose may we set Thee before us, and give us the assurance that all our plans are well-pleasing in Thy sight.

MARCUS DODS

455.

Almighty and eternal God, who on Easter Day didst turn the despair of the disciples into triumph of the resurrection of Christ who had been crucified, give us now assurance of Thy victory over evil and death within us and within our world.

O living Lord, whose touch makes all things new, make us sharers of Thy life, strong and free, glad and triumphant. Inspire in Thy people of America, of the world, energy of mind and spirit, that with courage and enthusiasm we may meet life eager and unafraid; in the power of Him who is more than conqueror in all things, Jesus Christ our Lord.

David A. MacLennan

456.

We pray to Thee, O Christ, to keep us under the spell of immortality.

May we never again think and act as if Thou wert dead. Let us more and more come to know Thee as a living Lord who hath promised to them that believe: "Because I live, ye shall live also."

Help us to remember that we are praying to the Conqueror of Death, that we may no longer be afraid nor be dismayed by the world's problems and threats, since Thou hast overcome the world.

In Thy strong name, we ask for Thy living presence and Thy victorious power.

Peter Marshall

457.

Dear heavenly Father, help us always to keep Easter in our hearts, to walk in its sunlight, to rejoice in its beauty, to live in its victory. Thou hast been good to us, infinitely good. Oh, make us now truly thankful to Thee. Take away our sin, our doubt, our shortsightedness. Widen for us the perspective of life. Make us to know that neither life nor death, nor things present nor things to come, nor height nor depth nor any other creature shall be able to separate us from Thy love in Christ Jesus.

Bring unto the sorrowing all release from pain. Let the cup of laughter overflow again. Set Thy love, like a burning beacon, over against the darkness and grief of life, to lighten our path and to bring us at last to Thee. At eventide may we commune with Thee again. Then finally may we see Thee as Thou art and in Thy presence, redeemed and glorified and made at home in heaven, may we abide forever. We ask it all, conscious of no merit in ourselves, but resting secure upon that hope which Christ has given in His resurrection on Easter Day.

Gerhard E. Lenski

Index of Contributors and Sources

(Item numbers are listed.)

Index of Poetry

(Titles, first lines, and poets are listed by poem numbers. Titles are in italics.)

218

Index of Subjects

(Item numbers are listed.)

220